Social Entrepreneurship
in Education

New Frontiers in Education
A Rowman & Littlefield Education Series
Edited by Dr. Frederick M. Hess

This Rowman & Littlefield Education series provides educational leaders, entrepreneurs, and researchers the opportunity to offer insights that stretch the boundaries of thinking on education.

Educational entrepreneurs and leaders have too rarely shared their experiences and insights. Research has too often been characterized by impenetrable jargon. This series aims to foster volumes that can inform, educate, and inspire aspiring reformers and allow them to learn from the trials of some of today's most dynamic doers; provide researchers with a platform for explaining their work in language that allows policymakers and practitioners to take full advantage of its insights; and establish a launch pad for fresh ideas and hard-won experience.

Whether an author is a prominent leader in education, a researcher, or an entrepreneur, the key criterion for inclusion in *New Frontiers in Education* is a willingness to challenge conventional wisdom and pat answers.

The series editor, Frederick M. Hess, is the director of education policy studies at the American Enterprise Institute and can be reached at rhess@aei.org or (202) 828-6030.

Other titles in the series:

Working for Kids: Educational Leadership as Inquiry and Invention
    By James H. Lytle

It's the Classroom, Stupid: A Plan to Save America's Schoolchildren
    By Kalman R. Hettleman

Choosing Excellence in Public Schools: Where There's a Will, There's a Way
    By David W. Hornbeck with Katherine Conner

Social Entrepreneurship in Education

Private Ventures for the Public Good

Michael R. Sandler

ROWMAN & LITTLEFIELD EDUCATION

A division of

ROWMAN & LITTLEFIELD PUBLISHERS, INC.
Lanham • New York • Toronto • Plymouth, UK

Published by Rowman & Littlefield Education
A division of Rowman & Littlefield Publishers, Inc.
A wholly owned subsidiary of The Rowman & Littlefield Publishing Group, Inc.
4501 Forbes Boulevard, Suite 200, Lanham, Maryland 20706
http://www.rowmaneducation.com

Estover Road
Plymouth PL6 7PY
United Kingdom

British Library Cataloguing in Publication Information Available

Library of Congress Cataloging-in-Publication Data

Sandler, Michael R., 1940-
  Social entrepreneurship in education : private ventures for the public good / Michael R. Sandler.
    p. cm. — (New frontiers in education)
  Includes bibliographical references and index.
  ISBN 978-1-60709-355-8 (cloth : alk. paper) — ISBN 978-1-60709-356-5 (pbk. : alk. paper) — ISBN 978-1-60709-357-2 (electronic)
  1. Business and education—United States.   2. Privatization in education—United States.   I. Title.
  LC1085.2.S26 2010
  371.19'5—dc22   2009034212

Printed in the United States of America

⊗™ The paper used in this publication meets the minimum requirements of American National Standard for Information Sciences—Permanence of Paper for Printed Library Materials, ANSI/NISO Z39.48-1992.

Table of Contents

Acknowledgments

This book could not have been written without the help of many people who shared my entrepreneurial journey in the education industry. First, I wish to thank my family for their steadfast support. My wife, Ellen, who has been my rock, best friend, and advisor and our daughters, Marcy, Susan, and Amy, and their families who have been there for me every step of the way. I would like to thank my brother, Jerry, who has helped me with the editing as a published author himself in his field of medicine. I also want to thank my colleagues who worked closely with me on this book. The "team" consisted of Lenore Ealy, Shannon Murphy-Farley, and Amy Sandler. They helped to keep me on track, which was no small challenge. I particularly want to thank my assistant, Sherry Campbell, who has met every deadline on time with a smile and unwavering support. Special thanks to Tom Koerner, whose sensitive and constructive guidance provided me with the motivation to clarify my focus and direction. I wish to thank my editors at American Enterprise Institute, Rick Hess who literally wrote the book on entrepreneurship in education and Juliet Squire, who were always there when called upon. I also want to thank my colleagues from the Education Industry Association, Steve Pines and Chris Yelich. I would like to thank my longtime associates, Gib Hentscheke and Jay MacLaughlin. In addition, I wish to thank my colleagues at Eduventures Inc., Peter Stokes, Sean Gallagher, and former Eduventurites Katherine Rynearson and Ian Cohen. I also wish to thank Roger Porter, Scott Leland, Miranda Daniloff Mancusi, and Bill Symonds of Harvard's Kennedy School Center for Business and Government. Finally, I wish to say a special thanks to my friends and family who encouraged and enthusiastically supported my pursuit of social entrepreneurship in education.

Preface

Entrepreneurs are essential drivers of innovation and progress. In the business world, they act as engines of growth, harnessing opportunity and innovation to fuel economic advancement. Social entrepreneurs act similarly, tapping inspiration and creativity, courage and fortitude, to seize opportunities that challenge and forever change established, but fundamentally inequitable systems.

—Skoll Foundation

Social entrepreneurship is not a new phenomenon, but it is has taken on heightened urgency in today's increasingly interconnected world of "haves" and "have-nots." It is a phrase on the tips of tongues of students, educators, and policy makers from Berkeley to Cambridge and everywhere in between—including Cairo, Egypt, in a speech by President Barack Obama in June 2009. There is a growing wave of people working around the world leveraging entrepreneurial principles to solve public problems and make social change.

Public education in the United States is one of those "established, but fundamentally inequitable systems" that social entrepreneurs have set their sights on. The recent surge in applications for Teach for America, the KIPP Academies, and other charter schools shows the growing hunger among young people to contribute to the public good and improve education. But this burgeoning interest by the next generation to work within the traditional educational structure is not the beginning of the story . . .

Since the report *A Nation at Risk* was released in 1983, there has been a growing class of "education entrepreneurs"—social entrepreneurs whose mission was to improve educational outcomes for students across America.

These entrepreneurs established meaningful and successful enterprises and are responsible for the creation and growth of one of the most important sectors in the U.S. economy—the education industry.

These entrepreneurs worked inside and around the traditional education infrastructure to bolster the learning experiences of millions of students in new and innovative ways. If today's educators, administrators, and public policy makers are to maximize the energy and resources of the new generation of social entrepreneurs in education, it would be helpful to understand the successes and pitfalls of the generation that came before.

This book tells the story of those who came before—the "education entrepreneurs" who toiled beneath the radar for years and created private ventures for the public good. Mixing never-before-shared, first-hand accounts, company and personal profiles, and enterprise and industry data, *Social Entrepreneurship in Education* illuminates the many possibilities for non-traditional business approaches to education. It is a must read for those trying to understand how social entrepreneurship can work to effectively, efficiently, and successfully improve education for American students.

We are on the cusp of huge changes in the education industry. It is forecasted to grow significantly from its $100 billion base, spurred mostly by new learning models on the Internet and the merging of Web 2.0 and social learning. Just as change has happened to the automotive industry and the financial services industry, so too is change coming to education. As we are seeing in districts across the country, change is in. It is in for students, for businesspeople, and it will have to be "in" for superintendents and other administrators.

The book is divided into three sections. The first explores the motivations behind why someone from the private sector would choose to operate within the existing education system and how to do so innovatively and efficiently. The second section details the trials and tribulations of an education entrepreneur working to build a scalable and profitable research and consulting business, while simultaneously helping to define and build infrastructure for a still-nascent education industry. The final section provides a broad look at the investment history in the industry, particularly the boom-and-bust period in the dot-com era and the overall impact of the Internet on education. It is from this period that many of the new breed of education entrepreneurs evolved and a sustainable industry sector was established.

The book surveys what has been done in the past twenty-five years and what lies ahead, now that the foundation for social entrepreneurship in education has been created. This is not intended to be a policy book. It is a book that tells the stories of the innovators who defined an industry and the characteristics they share as "education entrepreneurs." It is a story about passion and perseverance, about people who wanted to grow businesses while giving back to society. In many ways, this is a story about the American Dream and the many people who remain committed to making a better life for our nation's children. While we still may be "A Nation At Risk," this book takes an optimistic look at our future. The people you will meet in the following pages show us that even during challenging times, we can regain our position as the leader in education at home and around the world.

But all of us must recognize that education and innovation will be the currency of the 21st century . . . I am emphasizing such investments within my country . . . On education, we will expand exchange programs, and increase scholarships, like the one that brought my father to America . . . invest in online learning for teachers and children around the world; and create a new online network, so a teenager in Kansas can communicate instantly with a teenager in Cairo . . . All of us share this world for but a brief moment in time. The question is whether we spend that time focused on what pushes us apart, or whether we commit ourselves to an effort—a sustained effort—to find common ground, to focus on the future we seek for our children, and to respect the dignity of all human beings.

—President Barack Obama, June 4, 2009, Cairo, Egypt

Chapter 1

Energy and Persistence
Conquer All Things

Chapter 1 sets the stage for describing why a private entrepreneur would want to wander into the wilderness of social entrepreneurship in education. It explores the particularly complicated world of education entrepreneurship, located as it is at the intersection of both business and the public sector, and shows the importance of gaining an understanding of the various coalitions of stakeholders and their interests and the important needs of alignment for a successful outcome. The chapter title foreshadows some of the unique characteristics of a social entrepreneur in education.

Americans are a restless breed. We're not complacent. We like to think we can create and control our own destiny, while tinkering and fixing as opportunities and challenges arise. And that strand of our history is as present in our nation's approach to education as it is anywhere. People come to America to make better lives for themselves, and lives better still for their children. This hope largely springs from the American ideal of quality education for all.

But in practice, this ideal has largely fallen short. More than a quarter of a century ago, on April 26, 1983, the National Commission on Excellence in Education released their now-famous report on the U.S. education system, *A Nation at Risk*. The report identified myriad, systemic problems and noted a "rising tide of mediocrity" in our system that was allowing other countries to meet and even surpass America's educational, industrial, and commercial achievements. The authors asserted that had a foreign power attempted to impose such mediocrity on our schools and students, Americans "might well have viewed it as an act of war."

But the Commission also found reason for optimism. In their letter of transmittal to the Secretary of Education, the Commission wrote:

> The Commission deeply believes that the problems we have discerned in American education can be both understood and corrected if the people of our country, together with those who have public responsibility in the matter, care enough and are courageous enough to do what is required.

It was against this national backdrop of sustained concern with education that a groundswell for the creation of what eventually became the foundation of an "education industry" began. Many people, particularly those with entrepreneurial instincts, began to recognize that education was a sector of the economy in flux and ripe for new ideas. These entrepreneurs, together with visionary educators, administrators, and policymakers, have made up the corps of people in the past quarter century who have begun to "do what was required," as the Commission wrote, to bring education and the education industry into the 21st century.

The time was ripe for utilizing private sector skills and experience to create public good.

KENNEDY SCHOOL FELLOWSHIP

The Business Fellows Program at the Harvard Kennedy School's Center for Business and Government, led by Professor John Dunlop, offered an opportunity to meld a private sector background with a future focused on the public good. Dunlop, a labor economist and former presidential adviser and labor secretary, sought to infuse the Center for Business and Government with "real world" practitioners who could explore issues at the nexus of the public and private sectors. These practitioners were business fellows, and in 1989 their work and research focused on topics as diverse as finance, healthcare, energy, and telecommunications.

Amidst the growing national conversation concerning the American education system, the Center had identified education and its relationship with the private sector as one of its research priorities. As an entrepreneur with an interest in education, the fall of 1989 was a perfect time to consider issues in education and how the private sector could serve as a partner and resource for solving some of its thorniest problems.

Harvard's Kennedy School crackles with energy and passion and curiosity. While everybody is friendly and collegial, the environment is competitive. Professor Dunlop hosted a weekly brown bag lunch series where senior faculty members discussed a paper or case study on a topic relevant to the intersection of public and private interests. One faculty member was assigned to present the paper or case; another would argue a different point of view. Attendees were regularly exposed to an extraordinary array of distinguished scholars, including: Raymond Vernon (Clarence Dillon Professor of International Affairs Emeritus), Roger Porter (IBM Professor of Business and Government and currently the Center's director), Robert Glauber (former undersecretary of the Treasury for finance), Bill Hogan (Raymond Plank Professor of Global Energy Policy), Robert Lawrence (Albert L. Williams Professor of International Trade and Investment) and Robert Reich (former U.S. labor secretary).

Attending these lunches offered the chance to develop listening and observation skills, which ended up being one of the most valuable lessons of the fellowship. These skills would be particularly necessary to build the broad constituency support required to achieve reforms in education. The Kennedy School used meals to facilitate conversation and debate, feeding minds ahead of bodies; another example of how an informal and collegial setting can enhance the learning process, much as the traditional golf game can facilitate the negotiation of a business deal.

Sitting in on those lunches and observing some of the greatest minds tackle the problems of the day, it quickly became clear that many policy issues were neither clearly defined nor easily resolved, particularly in education. Hearing both sides build compelling cases for differing points of view helped both participants and visitors understand that the public policy process is rife with complexity. It is a different kind of complexity from that found in business. In business, you define your model, determine competition and strategy, build your team, and execute. But it seemed that every good policy idea at the intersection of business and government had some area of conflict with a different constituency. Whether it was bank regulation, clean energy, or international trade, there were clear plusses and minuses on both sides of the argument. Becoming aware of and attuned to that unavoidable complexity is a prerequisite for anyone trying to further items on a policy reform agenda.

STARTING THE JOURNEY

By 1989, it was evident that the enormous scale of the national education enterprise, in all its dimensions, offered interesting challenges, and at that time, high-quality, relevant research about any type of education "industry" was difficult to obtain, even in light of *A Nation at Risk*. In fact, Harvard's Kennedy School offered no courses on the subject. In 1989, an education industry was still in its earliest stages of formulation, and the role of business was viewed solely as a supportive partner and not as a driving force in its own right. Then, as now, schools of education were somewhat skeptical of private sector contributions to education. Business schools largely avoided focusing on education due to the political nature of its execution. The Center for Business and Government at the Kennedy School offered a unique opportunity to focus on this public policy problem in a more neutral light, allowing space for both public and private contributions in education.

Business schools avoided focusing on education because of political complexities, but at the Center for Business and Government there were individuals who identified the possible contributions the private sector could make to education. Dick Cavanagh, the executive dean of the Kennedy School, a former senior partner at McKinsey, and author of a bestselling management book, *The Winning Performance,* thought it worthwhile to identify how entrepreneurs could make optimum contributions to education.

Cavanagh taught a class on entrepreneurship in the public sector. It was his analysis of the characteristics of successful public entrepreneur Robert Moses, whom he called America's "first public entrepreneur," that was most fascinating. Moses, though not without much controversy, almost single-handedly transformed New York City by creating infrastructure connecting all five boroughs of city, thus linking America's biggest city for commerce and social interactivity. Before Moses, there was no Triborough Bridge, no Jones Beach State Park, no Verrazano Narrows Bridge, no West Side Highway, no Long Island parkway system, nor the Niagara or St. Lawrence power projects. Moses was not a professional planner by training—he was a political scientist who used his expertise and education for what he envisioned as the public good. Moses exemplified the possibilities for entrepreneurial energies to be applied to create public value.

Because of the ideological and institutional legacy of education in America, education entrepreneurs have had to work in the interstices of business and government and navigate the difficult waters where private and public interests converge. The most successful education entrepreneurs have needed to exhibit the characteristics Cavanagh discerned in the career of Robert Moses: passion, drive, focus, and a visionary's clarity about the future. The challenging terrain of education requires a sort of zealotry—a single-mindedness of purpose almost to the point where being called crazy is not considered an insult.

One of the few examples of education researchers at Harvard at that time was Paul Peterson, director of the Program on Education Policy and Governance. He now serves as a member of the independent review panel advising the Department of Education's evaluation of the No Child Left Behind law. Peterson's research focuses on school choice and vouchers, which The Editorial Projects in Education Research Center says is among the country's most influential studies of education policy. Meeting Peterson and studying his work offered an appreciation for the importance of education research, something that would be underscored in future experiences.

By organizing a series of seminars on the role of entrepreneurship in the public sector, with a specific focus on education, a steady stream of innovators who worked at the nexus of business and government were brought through the Kennedy School. Students at the Kennedy School were there to prepare for public service, to work in the government or in a not-for-profit field. Those with an entrepreneurial itch who wanted to create or build new enterprises typically enrolled at Harvard Business School instead. This seminar series exposed students to individuals who worked with a foot in each sector, or navigated back and forth between the two.

The four guest speakers were people who had proven records of entrepreneurial leadership in state, local, or federal government, as well as leaders in not-for-profits and foundations. Presenters told their stories creating and managing "public sector" enterprises with the same strict accountability the private sector required. While profit was not the primary motive, all had been responsible for the generation of additional and new sources of revenue. John Silber, the cantankerous and controversial president of Boston University at the time, who would go on to lead one of the most innovative school reform projects in the 1990s, presented his vision for education reform in Chelsea, Massachusetts.

Another memorable seminar was taught by Brian Carty, the director of the Commonwealth of Massachusetts Finance Agency, which had established a group of low-cost capital funds to invest in enterprises in the cities and towns with the highest unemployment rates in the state. Some of the students followed up on his presentation and gained experience by volunteering to help the state agency in its implementation.

Josiah (Joe) Spaulding Jr., who, at that time, had recently left Great Woods, a for-profit event and entertainment business, to run the newly established non-profit Wang Center of Performing Arts, outlined his plans to take the start-up to $10 million in revenue in five years, which he eventually did. Joe recently reflected on his vision and commitment to success:

> I'm an entrepreneur. Entrepreneurs usually don't sit in a CEO seat for any period of time in the same business . . . The constant challenge is creating a successful business model for a particular time. In 1987, we [the Wang Center] were about to be bulldozed down . . . When we started our educational outreach program, I went to a seventh grade classroom and asked the students, 'How many of you think the arts are important?' Nobody raised a hand. Then I asked, 'Do you sing in the shower? Do you go to the movies? Do you read books? Do you carry your boom box and listen to music? Do you like to do these things?' They all nodded. Then I asked the question again and every hand went up. You

can make that same speech at The Chamber of Commerce on the same day and get exactly the same result."

Joe Spaulding is a genuine public entrepreneur who stayed with his model and truly made a difference by expanding access to the performing arts. His creativity in developing a sustainable business model for something unique (the performing arts) inspired me to believe that similar efforts could be made in education. The students who participated at the seminar connected with his enthusiasm and were truly inspired. Jay Kislak, from the Miami chapter of the Young Presidents' Organization (YPO), who had recently accepted a position to head a department in the U.S. Department of Agriculture, offered a very frank view of the outcomes and challenges of working in a federal government agency.

The highlight of the seminars was the final meeting where we discussed an overview of our findings and identified areas of particular interest to the students. Students engaged in a lively discussion of the similarities and differences of the entrepreneurial characteristics of each presenter and the capacity for scale and replication of their endeavors.

During this final session, an impersonator of America's first entrepreneur, Benjamin Franklin, spoke. Boston-born Franklin was not only a Founding Father, but also a scientist, politician, diplomat, writer, and printer. He was the author of some of the most famous quotes used in our everyday lives. During the session, many of these quotes were discussed, and the group chose "Energy and Persistence Conquer All Things" as one that they felt most inspires entrepreneurs. That quote has become a familiar mantra for many education entrepreneurs and common characteristics mentioned in this book.

Among Professor Dunlop's many extraordinary gifts was his knack for creative problem solving. He was widely regarded as a world-class labor negotiator, and his talent for problem solving came from his virtuoso negotiating skills. Because of these uncommon gifts, Professor Dunlop served in numerous advisory positions throughout his career. In the 1980s, he sat on a panel created by then-Massachusetts Governor Michael Dukakis regarding the possible management of the Chelsea, Massachusetts, public schools by Boston University. Chelsea was located just northeast of Boston and had once been a thriving town with one of the finest school systems in Massachusetts. By the 1980s, however, it had developed overwhelming fiscal problems, with many of its inhabitants moving to live in the suburbs and leaving the city with little in the way of business or industry. Discussions were underway for Boston University to take a leadership role in managing the school system to achieve true reform.

Professor Dunlop believed John Silber would offer a new and educational experience through his endeavors in Chelsea. He was correct, and participating in the Chelsea partnership offered a unique opportunity to watch a K-12 education reform effort firsthand. Dunlop's suggestion also underscored an important lesson that successful entrepreneurs learn early—trust your instincts with people you trust.

To contribute to the Chelsea project, Silber had asked for a proposal on a single sheet of paper. This resulted in the proposal for the creation of an independent foundation to support Boston University's educational priorities in Chelsea. Silber liked the concept, and plans were made to take it forward. The time spent as a fellow at Harvard and my hosting a seminar series exploring entrepreneurship in the public sector made it possible to present the proposal to Silber. The project clearly was a real-world practicum for testing the theoretical research offered by the Kennedy School. The Harvard experience exemplified the importance of taking time to think *and execute* outside the box—defining entrepreneurial traits to be sure.

GIVING BACK

Several years after my fellowship at Harvard, it was clear that other executives from the burgeoning education industry could similarly benefit from a year to reflect on their experiences and explore new paths. By establishing a business and education fellowship program, other entrepreneurs were provided with important learning, mentoring, and networking opportunities.

There have been three Sandler fellows to date. Each has repaid his fellowship with material contributions to research, teaching, and policy-making. Steven F. Wilson was the first. As the founder and president of Ascend Learning, Steve is now working to develop a scalable solution to the underachievement of economically disadvantaged children. While a fellow, he completed a book based on his experiences as the president of a chain of for-profit charter schools called Advantage Schools. The book *Learning on The Job; When Business Takes on Public Schools* was very instructive for future education entrepreneurs.

Dr. John Ebersole was the second fellow. John had previously been an associate provost at Boston University and dean of its Continuing Education School. John was interested in distance learning and studied the distinctions between for- profit and not-for-profit schools that established online learning programs. His work has become widely read by colleges and universities considering online programs. After John's fellowship at the Kennedy School, he was named president of Excelsior College in Albany, New York. Excelsior is the largest college in the United States, providing distance learning education courses to the U.S. Armed Forces.

The most recent fellow was Bill Symonds, who was the former education editor for *Business Week* magazine. Bill had written prolifically on the education industry and was the first to track education as a major sector of the U.S. economy. Bill's fellowship project has been to convene a series of executive sessions on the role of business and education in the 21st century. He has organized a Who's Who list of business, academic, and policy leaders to participate.

The experience at Harvard offered preparation for other lessons in public sector entrepreneurship. Being a fellow at the Center for Business and Government also provided a better understanding of the issues of business and education by discussing those issues with other business fellows at the Center. By experiencing firsthand the potential of business supporting education, it was clear that the same theories and practices could be applied to business and education. The theoretical lessons of ambiguity in the public policy process were soon to become a reality in the gritty real world challenges of the blighted Chelsea school system.

Chapter 2

Bold Interventions

While Chapter 1 outlines issues in education from a more academic environment, Chapter 2 focuses on the hands-on experience of trying to navigating the K-12 education sector as an outsider. It illustrates the challenges and obstacles of a leader of a traditional higher education institution attempting to solve a social problem of an underperforming K-12 school system through bold interventions by utilizing the leverage of a well-known university to assume management and responsibility for higher achieving outcomes. The issues and challenges arising from an unprecedented partnership between an impoverished city school district and a private university are explored in-depth. The chapter illustrates the remarkable changes that one individual with steel will and persistence can make in a situation deemed untouchable by the majority of the education establishment.

Boston University's Chelsea initiative was a landmark undertaking in 1989, unprecedented in its scope. This initiative reflected the opportunities for dramatic response to the call to arms from *A Nation at Risk.* A convergence of the issues and needs Chelsea presented, together with the growing national conversation on school reform, coincided with an increasing interest in dedicating my skills and resources to education. Chelsea was a laboratory where it was possible to combine a lifetime of entrepreneurial spirit and skill with academic theories.

Entrepreneurs, public or private, should never stop learning. Working in Chelsea provided just that opportunity to work *and* learn, while toiling directly under one of the country's leading public entrepreneurs, Boston University President John Silber. Dr. Silber's reputation preceded him, since he helped build Boston University into a leading academic institution, and it would be fascinating to learn how he planned to tackle this enormous challenge

Boston University's commitment to manage the Chelsea public school system was historic—it was the first third-party contract to manage public schools in America. The city of Chelsea itself had a dire financial condition and required not only leadership to support its schools, but also fiscal guidance to help the city improve over the long-term.

Chelsea was interesting because in addition to being located a scant 1.9 miles across the Mystic River from Boston, it was a microcosm of what America was evolving to look like in the 21st century. At the time, the city's population was 28,000 inhabitants. The school student body population was diverse—of the 3,700 matriculating students, 6 percent were African-American, 12 percent were Asian, 55 percent were Hispanic, and the remaining 27 percent were Caucasian. Income levels were remarkably low; 47 percent of households earned less than $10,000 annually (the national poverty threshold for a family of four in 1989 was $12,674). Only 44 percent of citizens had earned a high school diploma. The schools in Chelsea employed 242 teachers and budgeted $4,250 per student annually. No new schools had been built there since 1915, leaving sagging infrastructure and inadequate facilities. A staggering 52 percent of students dropped out before graduation. Only 10 percent of those who did graduate went on to four-year colleges. One quarter of the high school girls were either pregnant or already mothers.

The Chelsea initiative was no ordinary feat—a community had never invited a university to run its school system before. But by the late 1980s, some school districts were amenable to experimenting with new ways to achieve school reform and improvement. Chelsea's elected school committee selected Boston University to serve as manager, and it was agreed that going forward, the contract between the two entities could be terminated by a simple majority vote of the school committee. School committee meetings were open to the public and there was broad community input and support throughout the whole process.

Although the official date of the agreement between the city of Chelsea and Boston University was in 1989, conversations about the possibility of a third-party takeover of the city's schools had been ongoing for years. Behind closed doors, Dr. Silber and the late Andrew Quigley, former mayor of Chelsea and then-editor of the city's newspaper the *Chelsea Record,* had conducted a running conversation about the prospect of Boston University's sweeping involvement since 1983. In this same period in the mid-eighties, Dr. Silber also had made several unsuccessful proposals to run the city of Boston's school system. Seeing area schools as a prime arena for improvement, Silber believed the resources and "fresh eyes" of Boston University could make an important impact.

While Dr. Silber had worked for many years behind the scenes with former Mayor Quigley to support Chelsea, it wasn't until the city's parents gathered on November 29, 1988, that the agreement could officially move forward. Professor Dunlop had emphasized the importance of building diverse coalitions for a common objective; this was reconfirmed throughout the Chelsea engagement. The Boston University/Chelsea partnership resulted from the convergence of dire economic circumstances that left little alternative and was based upon an understanding that Boston University's offer was a last chance opportunity. Even the teachers' union, which was initially opposed to the program, read the landscape and came to share this sentiment as well. The union even ended up supporting some of the more entrepreneurial ideas that were offered by the Boston University team.

A DIFFERENT SEPTEMBER FOUNDATION (ADSF)

Boston University needed additional financial resources to implement their ideas and initiatives. Identifying and soliciting the donors necessary to do so would prove challenging. Thankfully, complex and thorny challenges are enticing to entrepreneurial problem solvers. The decision to establish an independent 501(c)3 foundation to support the work Boston University was undertaking in the city provided such an entrepreneurial opportunity. Its autonomous structure afforded the necessary freedom and opportunity needed to think creatively and execute efficiently. The establishment of the foundation served to reassure donors to the partnership that their funds would go directly to the Boston University/Chelsea initiative and not to other BU programs. One of the main challenges would be to build trust with the Chelsea business community and rally the parents of Chelsea. They needed to believe that Boston University was there to help.

The first task was to create a plan and structure for a development organization separate and distinct from the University's general fundraising offices. For a number of reasons, the Chelsea schools' needs had to be a distinct fundraising effort from those of the University at large. It was critical to assure donors that their gifts went directly to the schools. A separate, independent foundation would differentiate itself from other Boston University fundraising efforts.

A Different September Foundation (ADSF)—the independent 501(c)3 foundation to support the Boston University/Chelsea School partnership—was established for this purpose. This name appeared in the original proposal to Dr. Silber detailing an independent fundraising arm of the initiative. The name served to convey that through this work, the students of Chelsea *could* have a different September.

With the stroke of a pen, John Silber added A Different September Foundation to a university organizational chart, establishing it as one of four entities at the University reporting directly to the President's Office. This direct reporting relationship provided the autonomy necessary to succeed. Moreover, focused fundraising by a core group of individuals who understood the challenges and benefits of education reform would better serve the initiative than the Boston University Development Office.

Prior to ADSF's establishment, the University had raised approximately $3 million for the Chelsea initiative since the implementation of its contract in 1989. It had been successful in fundraising efforts with corporations and foundations and from individual donations from friends and trustees of the University. It was ADSF's responsibility to build upon the base and maintain those relationships while creating significant new opportunities. ADSF's staff of five was fully operational by January 1991.

ADSF's Advisory Board was comprised of leaders in education, business, and philanthropy as well as private-sector leaders and educators from the Chelsea community. The fundraiser's adage is that if you want advice, ask for money; if you want money ask for advice. Not only was ASDF asking for advice, but it was also doing crucial work in building awareness and opening lines of communication among centers of influence which had the power to broadcast our efforts in Chelsea to a national audience. Advisory Board members also utilized their own networks both locally and nationally to expand the scope of resources and support for Chelsea. Reaching out affirmatively to share successes and to ask for counsel and referrals from a broad network of demonstrated and potential friends of an enterprise is a sure way to drive toward goals and to market a project informally. A large and well-used contact list is the public entrepreneur's friend.

The Advisory Board significantly assisted ASDF's fundraising efforts early in its launch. They saw clearly that the Chelsea initiative was a major and novel effort contributing not just to the city of Chelsea, but to the improvement of American public education generally. They believed in the model of a university using its resources to help improve public schools, and they all understood that Boston University's involvement in this project was a long-term commitment and not a brief "experiment" that some in the press called it. ADSF's Advisory Board shared the University's dedication to stay with the program for the duration of its original ten-year contract, since true education reform of this magnitude could only be viewed in terms of decades, rather than years.

ADSF's original annual budget was $425,000. By June 30, 1991, it had raised $1,875,000, half of which came from fundraising activities done by the

Boston University Development Office prior to the establishment of ADSF. Every dollar raised by ADSF went directly to the Chelsea programs; the overhead was absorbed by the University to maximize donors' gifts. By good fortune and because of the broadly recognized importance of the project, ADSF was off to a good start, and it seemed that the model of an independent foundation to serve Chelsea's needs was correct.

ADSF's goals were narrowed to clearly mirror the fundraising objectives. It was crucial to develop fundraising priorities in conjunction with Boston University's goals for the Boston University/Chelsea Partnership.

The major themes of this Partnership were that:

• Children should be ready to learn.
• Teachers should be ready to teach.
• Something important must be taught.

The essence of a brand is repeated delivery on its promise over time. By creating these three simple objectives and keeping them in mind in all our communication and all our work, we tried to drive home the essence of Boston University's promise to Chelsea.

HOLISTIC LEARNING

In order to realize these goals, several important initiatives were launched to facilitate educational opportunities for all levels of the city's learners. This was also somewhat revolutionary to consider coupling noneducational ventures with school-based ones to achieve reform. One of the most important, supported early childhood education in the form of an early childhood learning center. This innovative program was open every working day of the year and provided day care in an educational environment for kindergartners and pre-kindergartners. Parents played an active role in the center, as they did in all parts of the Boston University/Chelsea partnership.

Early childhood learning was one of the most critical underpinnings of the partnership, and it reflected Dr. Silber's commitment to a long-term solution for Chelsea. Given the success of this endeavor, it was an area of interest to the press and one that garnered a good bit of publicity from the national media. Mary McGrory of the *Washington Post* came to Chelsea to visit the Early Learning Center.

On May 7, 1991, the *Washington Post* published McGrory's piece, entitled "Wrench in a Wheel of Poverty." It was an inspiring description of the Early Learning Center, a place where children were "reminded of their identity—and importance" in a room where their pictures hang on a wall, a map of Chelsea boasts ribbons marking their homes, and Mozart's Thirty-third Symphony plays in the background. McGrory wrote that "extended care is at the heart of this partnership between the city of Chelsea and Boston University. It is preschool wraparound, top of the line education for children at the bottom of the economic pile."

McGrory detailed Boston University's commitment to the project: "the school of social studies sends teams to the high school to intervene in violent outbreaks. The softball team paints out the gang graffiti . . . [and an] inter-generational literacy program helps immigrant parents learn to read English, while Boston University students mind their children in an adjoining room." McGrory understood the seriousness of the undertaking and the deep commitment of John Silber—the "brilliant and brusque president of Boston University" who "believes his program should serve as a model for the country." She ended her piece with the cautionary note that, "If a school system cannot be brought back to life with the flat-out effort of a major university and help from corporations, there is no hope."

Years later, in 2006, when Boston University wanted to honor Dr. Silber for his incredible efforts with the Chelsea schools, the University set about renaming the city's early childhood education center after him. The University recognized that early childhood education was Dr. Silber's greatest priority and even, perhaps, his greatest legacy. Since the early 1990s, the importance of early childhood education has become clear. But Dr. Silber and his team recognized its importance before it became a major national issue.

In addition to emphasizing early childhood education, Boston University and Chelsea began the Intergenerational Literacy Project with funding from the Xerox Corporation. It facilitated increasing adult literacy, using books that older family members could then read to children. The program also helped teach family members to speak English if it was not their first language. In 1990, seventy-four families were enrolled in this project. A year later witnessed a nearly 100 percent increase to 130 families.

Another major effort Dr. Silber identified as important to creating a readiness to learn was to support the delivery of quality healthcare. While Massachusetts General Hospital (MGH) had established a satellite facility in Chelsea, Boston University wanted to link these initiatives with their Schools of Medicine, Dentistry, and Law. A mobile dental clinic made regular visits to Chelsea, as many of its students had never seen a dentist. Boston University Medical School also supported the MGH facility in Chelsea by offering their students and residents an opportunity to provide volunteer support.

REPLICABILITY

One of ADSF's earliest objectives was to institutionalize its major programs and efforts to help financially sustain Boston University's activities throughout the original ten-year period of the contract. For some, it was also important that the community outreach of ADSF have a scalable model, should other higher educational institutions wish to replicate its work. This question of replication was a major challenge because it could have detracted from most efficiently attaining ADSF's goals for Chelsea. Because of the uniqueness of the Boston University/Chelsea Schools' partnership, it was important to focus our priorities on Chelsea and treat replication as a separate but important by-product of the results achieved there.

The issue of replication became an important area of discussion when planning fundraising priorities. After a cursory review, it was clear that few universities were willing to consider the liability of managing an entire school district while dealing with their own financial priorities. Dr. Silber had discussed this issue of K-12 school management for many years with his board, and they were supportive and understood the full implications. Other universities dipping their toes in the pool were learning about K-12 school management for the first time and were more cautious.

It was validating that in subsequent years, other universities such as Clark University in Worcester, Massachusetts and the University of Pennsylvania in Philadelphia led by Susan Fuhrman, have used their resources to support K-12 charter schools in their own neighborhoods. Success in Chelsea made these similar programs more possible, demonstrating that a good model and proven success itself can offer examples ripe for replication.

ADSF also needed to build additional coalitions of support within Boston University itself, so the Foundation reached out to the other schools within the University. The University's School of Communication offered its support by helping to develop a newsletter, logos, marketing materials, and annual reports. ADSF's public relations efforts were planned and executed in conjunction with the University's Public Affairs Office. Boston University's School of Education was the major partner representing Boston University in Chelsea and among other services offered teacher training and professional development programs for the school administrators, demonstrating their commitment to ensure that teachers were ready to teach.

By late 1991, successful fundraising earned ADSF credibility with its various constituencies and stakeholders. It also served as a main communications vehicle between the University and the Chelsea community. ADSF distributed a regular newsletter that included frequent updates on current activities and provided heads of programs and school administrators with an opportunity to explain their work and objectives in greater detail. This was crucial because the people in Chelsea had often felt that they were not included in the planning and direction of the partnership. The quarterly newsletter served as a very important communications vehicle, drawing in diverse constituencies, allowing them to feel informed, engaged, and part of the process. While ADSF was first and foremost a fundraising organization, it also operated in the key role of communications link between the Boston University team and the Chelsea community. Opening lines of communication among stakeholders is invaluable in the entrepreneurial process as different initiatives are undertaken, explored, executed, and discarded or advanced.

FALSE STARTS

Chelsea had not always known such difficult times as it experienced in the late-1980s and early-1990s. The city's halcyon years were in the 1940s, 1950s, and early-1960s. Small businesses in Chelsea had done well and the city felt a sense of pride for their well-regarded schools and athletic teams. Many Chelsea graduates were accepted at some of the finest universities in the Boston area, including Harvard and MIT. The makeup of Chelsea at that time was primarily first- or second-generation Americans who were Irish, Italian, Polish, or Jewish.

Many of these alumni of the Chelsea schools had a strong affinity to the city, so much so that each year while they were on their winter vacations in Florida, a group organized an annual Chelsea high school reunion event. Potential donors said that this group of seniors had very fond memories of Chelsea and would be likely prospects to support the reform through ADSF. Interestingly, a fundraising trip to visit alumni in Florida yielded little.

Since the fundraising results were miniscule, Dr. Silber's reaction was one of great disappointment. But then, as with other risky ventures, it was evident that while not every good idea succeeds, it is worth taking risks. The Chelsea retirees were more interested in nostalgia than giving money. On the face of it, they were likely prospects, but they had no current vested interest in Chelsea, riddled as it was with financial and social problems. The group wanted to reminisce rather than get involved. Another lesson learned.

BUILDING CONFIDENCE AND BUY-IN

Included in the process of building lines of communication, awareness, and hopefully a coalition of supporters was the creation of a local community group. ADSF reached out to younger business and community leaders, as well as school administrators and teachers in Chelsea and solicited their time and counsel. The objective was to develop as many differing constituencies as possible that were all aligned to help the children of Chelsea and its community.

As we were reaching out, others were reaching out to us. The Chelsea Partnership had that effect on people, and one such person was Allan Afrow, General Counsel of Cumberland Farms Convenient Stores and himself a graduate of the Chelsea schools. Afrow helped to create the Friends of A Different September Foundation, an affinity group to ADSF whose mission was to support the teachers, administrators, and employees of the Chelsea schools. At the first annual Friends of ADSF event, to build community the group honored teachers and had some of the local students make presentations and perform. The parents of the students who were invited to the event enthusiastically participated, so we knew this program would gain traction.

The local newspaper quoted Afrow's comments at the first official meeting of the Friends of ADSF, held at the Chelsea Public Library: "Chelsea gave me something to be proud of—it gave me sense of community. I've asked myself what can I do to help the city of Chelsea? . . . Not too long ago I was lying in a hospital very near death suffering from major heart failure and the thought entered my mind . . . what have I done in my life that has made a difference?" Afrow's volunteer service as Chairman of the Friends of ADSF added tremendous credibility and validation to its efforts, largely because of his own personal ties to the community.

To build on this positive start, ADSF tried to make all citizens of Chelsea understand they were stakeholders in the schools. There's a saying that racetracks make most of their money on $2 bettors. The foundation needed to make money *and* build consensus by including Chelsea's $2 bettors; expanding a donor base and increasing the number of citizens who felt they had a stake in the schools' success. Kevin White, the former mayor of Boston, and the director of Boston University's Institute for Political Communication helped promote a "Chelsea Schools stock certificate" with a minimum purchase of ten shares at $1.00 per share. Mr. White was a highly regarded mayor of Boston and responsible for its major economic development during his tenure in the 1980s.

White's presentation at a meeting in Chelsea was particularly interesting— he said that he was struck by the similarities between the cities of Chelsea and Boston. He commented that when Chelsea was booming in the 1940s and 1950s, Boston, just across the bridge, was in chaos, whereas now, Chelsea was a city in turmoil, while Boston enjoyed a certain amount of economic stability. Having Kevin White come to Chelsea and draw links between Chelsea and Boston and offer a positive attitude to the Chelsea business community received very favorable publicity. Though the purpose of the stock certificate was largely for publicity as well, it also achieved some moderately successful fundraising results, and most importantly, created the sense that the business community and parents were shareholders and stakeholders in this effort. The Friends of ADSF raised over $5,000 that night and, more importantly, brought in over more than 200 new donors—primarily Chelsea residents.

CONTINUOUS CHALLENGES

But for every success, such as the spontaneous generosity that led to forming the Early Childhood Center, there also were setbacks. Being prepared for setbacks was part of the job, since from the beginning the situation in Chelsea was fragile. In June 1991, the superintendent of Chelsea Schools, Diana Lam, resigned to run for mayor of the city of Boston. A setback and a disappointment to be sure, but prudent entrepreneurs know that in complex public policy initiatives on this scale, no one individual is indispensable—our momentum was not to be lost.

To fill the vacant superintendent position, Boston University reached out to its management team and appointed Peter Greer, dean of the Boston University School of Education, as interim superintendent of Chelsea Schools. In turn, Ted Sharpe, dean of the Education School, succeeded Peter as chairman. Diana Lam's mayoral campaign was short-lived. She returned to education, which was her true calling, to become superintendent, with varying degrees of success, in several urban school districts.

While the Chelsea schools' management team was unpaid, its members were some of the most competent, committed, and effective volunteers in the field, illustrating how personal dedication to an issue can serve as a powerful motivator to one's daily work. Members of the management team included Boston University faculty-experts in mathematics, languages and the arts, and healthcare. Also serving was the University's controller and labor relations attorney. In addition, one of the most active and supportive members of the management team was Dr. Robert Sperber, who was on the faculty of the Boston University School of Education, and a highly regarded former superintendent of schools in Brookline, Massachusetts.

Observing and participating in the meetings of the management team and the school board in Chelsea was an impressive experience, particularly because of the sincerity and professionalism of everyone involved. Most interesting was the transformation from skepticism to understanding and trust between the independent school board and the management team. Building these kinds of relationships in a stressful and skeptical environment, with an outside entity managing the schools in a city with significant financial uncertainty, is no small task. Relative transparency and candor went a long well to opening dialog and growing trust.

CHELSEA'S FINANCIAL ISSUES

The time invested in building this confidence and trust helped when dealing with one of the biggest issues facing Chelsea: the budget for fiscal year 1992. Chelsea Mayor John Brennan's new budget called for massive budget cuts for the schools. While Dr. Silber was in the midst of dealing with the replacement of the superintendent, he also attended a management meeting to discuss the budget issues in more detail. The stakes were high and the budget shortfall was enormous. In order for the city of Chelsea to have a balanced budget, the request by Boston University for operating expenses of $15.9 million (which was level from the prior year) was reduced to a proposal of $11.6 million. This would have resulted in a 39 percent reduction since Boston University had assumed management of the schools in 1989. The management meeting was an open public meeting, and when Dr. Silber arrived he was greeted with boos and cries to dump Boston University. The public outcry came as the mayor had just laid off twenty-three public safety workers, and their union and the teachers union formally organized a joint protest that had the potential to get out of control. With Diana Lam's departure and Chelsea's financial issues on the table, the influential local paper, the *Boston Globe*, began to weigh in, implying and suggesting that perhaps the University's partnership with Chelsea should be terminated.

By June 1991, the teachers couldn't be paid because the city was so strapped for cash that city officials asked Governor Weld for an advance on payments from the Commonwealth. In August, the Commonwealth recommended a receivership for the city. The Senate Committee made its recommendation in a report to the state Executive Office of Administration and Finance, which had been commissioned in June. The mayor of Chelsea was pleased, and said he felt vindicated, as this was what he had been requesting.

On September 12, 1991, then-Governor Weld made Chelsea the first Massachusetts municipality to enter receivership since the Great Depression. Weld swore in James Carlin, a successful businessman and the former state transportation secretary of the Commonwealth as Chelsea's overseer for a salary of a dollar a year. James Carlin immediately made the Chelsea school system his highest priority. Two days later the schools were due to open. In order to finance the opening of the schools, the receiver requested prepayment assistance of $4 million. This request was approved as the authority of the receiver had unprecedented scope. In a receivership situation, the receiver supersedes the city's mayor and has the power to unilaterally formulate budgets, issue bonds, and abrogate contracts. The receiver also reduces the Board of Aldermen to advisory status.

The story of Chelsea's reopening and the receivership drew national attention. *Education Week* covered the story extensively and reported on the financial mechanics of the process of the receivership. It also gave Boston University favorable grades on the actual outcomes achieved to that date. They cited data from their research that Chelsea scores on the SAT and state standardized tests had been improving and that Boston University's management team had made steady progress in building collaborative rather than combative relationships with the school committee.

This positive information was a turning point, one that could be an opportunity to develop further coalitions of support for Boston University and Chelsea. Having a receiver who was independent and clearly focused on financial stability—in contrast to being politically motivated—helped to create an environment that encouraged additional positive outcomes.

While the receiver was monitoring Chelsea's finances, the Chelsea Oversight Panel was grading Boston University. The Panel had been established by former Massachusetts Governor Michael Dukakis to evaluate Boston University's involvement in the sweeping school reform effort. In February 1992, the Panel published its report on the outcomes from the 1990–91 school year, the second year of the partnership. The Panel commended the partnership for its "impressive" fund raising for early childhood education, "exemplary programs" ranging from intergenerational literacy to social work, and "expanded involvement of teachers in educational planning and professional development activities."

The team was heartened and energized by the positive feedback but mindful that there were still enormous challenges ahead. The report described Boston University's efforts to develop a "more open, two-way communication system" with the community as laudable and representing continued progress. They noted that "the improvements made by the Boston University Management Team to reach out to the various constituencies in Chelsea needed to be continued, enhanced, and accelerated in light of the difficulties facing the school system and the city." They also cautioned that Boston University "must continue to attend to these issues . . . in view of many underlying attitudes and even hostilities in the community."

FOCUS AT A DIFFERENT SEPTEMBER FOUNDATION

The challenges that the Panel referred to were no surprise. While they had reached a crisis point resulting in the receivership, there were other cities in America whose public schools faced similar challenges. The offices of ADSF continually focused on ways to move the ball forward. Though ADSF's goals were not necessarily to create a replicable model, ADSF employees frequently thought beyond Chelsea and its financial issues to wider national policy concerns. ADSF developed a series of programs and outreach efforts to address the possibility of duplication of the Chelsea model and to share the lessons that were learned.

The first such program was at a conference on school reform funded by one of our major foundation supporters and hosted by the CEO, Harold McGraw of McGraw-Hill in New York. Presenters from Chelsea's management team discussed the performance of the Chelsea schools relative to its priorities, and some education policy-thought leaders were invited to discuss Chelsea and its potential for replication. There were approximately 200 attendees.

Because of the favorable publicity and positive reaction to presentations, the conference hosted by McGraw-Hill was a singular success. At the beginning of the conference, there was skepticism about Boston University's efforts in Chelsea—the work was viewed solely as a terminal experiment. We had seen this term "experiment" before, which connoted a lack of commitment on the part of Boston University—even though the University had made a ten-year commitment. By the end of the conference it was clear that not only was the partnership not an "experiment," as it had been pejoratively termed, but one that could leave a lasting impact on the city and children of Chelsea.

SUCCESSION PLANNING

Serial entrepreneurs are a particularly restless breed. This was—and is—a main challenge of being an entrepreneur who is motivated by starting and building new things and becomes bored with the daily routine. Such serial entrepreneurs must create forms of institutional memory and enduring brand continuity before moving on.

Dr. Silber and his political allies were already lobbying the Commonwealth for financial support to rebuild the structures of the remaining Chelsea schools. The newest school in Chelsea had been built in 1926. To support this effort, ADSF reproduced photos of all eight schools and developed a package of postcards, which we sent to all donors and used as thank-you notes.

This helped engage the community, and shortly after the city emerged from receivership, the new school construction plan was approved.

The dream came true in September 1996, when a truly different September occurred. A $116 million construction was approved—almost entirely at state expense. A new colorful brick complex was opened housing four elementary schools. The schools had a separate entrance but shared a library, playgrounds, gyms, and cafeterias. Two middle schools and a high school were also opened. *USA Today* covered the opening, and school board chair Morrie Seigal said, "I can't tell you how long we have waited for this day."

For the fiscal year 1991 ending June 30, 1992, ADSF raised an additional $2 million, to bring our totals to over $5 million in gifts since inception. It had a good staff in place and a long list of prospects and proposals pending. It also had momentum for at least one year, but to maintain that momentum, the task of finding a successor became the highest priority. Boston University's Development Office and its Human Resource department helped identify candidates. ADSF needed a leader and fundraiser with a real passion for education and a dedication to the mission and priorities ADSF stood for.

After a careful search, Willoughby "Wib" Walling was selected. Wib brought to the job a distinguished education background in conjunction with a unique combination of experience in urban education, fundraising, business, and government. A graduate of Stanford, he also earned advanced degrees from Harvard's Graduate School of Education and the Harvard Business School. He had also designed and implemented a nationally acclaimed program for high school dropouts in Harlem and Bedford-Stuyvesant. He was the right person at the right time.

Wib came on board as president of ADSF on June 1, 1992, and, given his background and experience, also joined the Boston University/Chelsea Management team. He did an excellent job for many years and brought the total of our fundraising efforts since inception to more than $10 million. Doug Sears, who was on the management team and dean of the School of Education, succeeded Wib when Boston University signed an agreement in 1997 to extend the partnership until 2003. In 2006, the ADSF merged back into Boston University's Development Office. After Silber ceased to be president of Boston University the decision was made to terminate the contract. In June 2008, after nearly two decades, and ten years longer than the original contract, the Boston University/Chelsea School partnership ended with Boston University returning the school districts and its management role to the residents of Chelsea.

The Boston University/Chelsea partnership could be considered a success for many reasons. It was largely a success in the context of the circumstances that Chelsea found itself in when Boston University commenced its partnership with the schools. In 1989, many of Chelsea's school children were attending neighboring city parochial schools for the quality of education and school. Citizens now feel they can rely on the public schools to provide good education in a safe environment for their children. Despite the city of Chelsea being categorized in the lowest economic bracket with regards to the Massachusetts Standardized Assessment Testing (MCAS), their testing scores are among the highest within their grouping, which includes cities such as Boston, Springfield, Holyoke, Lawrence, Fall River, and New Bedford. As of 2008, Chelsea has virtually all new schools and finds itself a safer and more fiscally solvent city. There is a genuine appreciation for what Boston University was able to accomplish in Chelsea

The experience in Chelsea during these years offered invaluable on-the-job training in education reform. The portability of entrepreneurial skills from the private sector was validated. The Boston University/Chelsea partnership exemplified that communication and consensus building, branding and effective marketing, and most surely, innovation are highly transferable skills from one sector to another. Raising capital for worthy causes and investments can be fulfilling both psychologically and financially.

Having Professor Dunlop engaged and interested in the Boston University/Chelsea partnership was a valued and reassuring resource and one that continued to stimulate imagining a different course for education in American cities. His involvement underscored the crucial role of mentorship in an entrepreneurial setting. Mentorship from Dunlop and Silber was, in many ways, complementary. They felt, though in different ways, that entrepreneurs could play a critical role in improving education.

The issues in Chelsea were much more complex than they appeared initially, and coalition building proved to be the critical foundation for long-term success. Developing close working relationships within the Boston University and Chelsea communities ended up making the job easier when things got tough—which it did, inevitably. Amid the heat and noise of passionate policy battles, focus on long-range, tangible goals is critical.

In public entrepreneurship, that singular focus is the primary driver and motivating force for success. In Dr. Silber's case, his drive was motivated by a passion to help the children of Chelsea. The fundraisers for the project were always ready and passionate about asking for money because we knew that we must not fail the children of Chelsea. Moments of crisis can help an organization to unite around a unifying goal and can provide the focus necessary for success.

Blazing new trails and creating new enterprises is the fulfillment of all entrepreneurs. Chelsea made clear that in K-12 education, entrepreneurial terrain is both tougher and more rewarding than many other challenges offered by business. With American schools in trouble across the nation, new sources and uses of capital—financial and entrepreneurial—had to be found. The challenge continues today.

Chapter 3

Breaking the Mold

Chapter 3 covers the challenges of K-12 education reform in an historic initiative by corporate America. This was the largest effort ever by the business community and had the full support of the president of the United States, but lays bare the limitations of private business in public education. Despite this effort to break the mold, it shows that even with near endless financial resources, and under the selfless leadership of David Kearns, true public education reform in America is a long term commitment that could be better served by entrepreneurs who are committed to devote their undivided time and resources given the enormous challenges they faced.

In the spring of 1991, as A Different September Foundation in Chelsea was being launched, President George H. W. Bush convened a meeting in the Smokey Mountains of Tennessee to facilitate "out of the box thinking" for a grand vision of education reform in America. This meeting resulted in the establishment of New American Schools Development Corporation. Eventually, "Development Corporation" was dropped from the end of the initiative's name because they wanted to convey a research and development operation, rather than a profit-generating entity. New American Schools (NAS) would also serve to be a groundbreaking initiative, as this corporate, philanthropic effort supported research and development for education innovation, which few others were doing at the time.

The meeting was historic because government officials seriously considered using a business approach to help improve public education—novel thinking at the time. The meeting was part of the continuing national dialogue on school reform that had been given such a jolt eight years earlier with the release of *A Nation at Risk* report. To many, this meeting was considered corporate America's response to the report's call to arms.

The business, government, and education policy leaders who attended the meeting discussed a variety of topics, such as: establishing a model school for every congressional school district, with distinct designs and programs that could be replicated; establishing private for-profit schools, which would compete with public schools; and even school choice and vouchers. Attendees included the former CEO of Xerox, David Kearns, who at the time was serving as deputy secretary of education, Secretary of Education Lamar Alexander, Governor Tom Keane of New Jersey, and his commissioner of education, Saul Cooperman, future statesman of education reform Chester (Checker) Finn, and Edison Schools founder Chris Whittle.

CHELSEA SCHOOLS PARTNERSHIP AND NEW AMERICAN SCHOOLS COMPARISON

The goal of New American Schools was to achieve urgently needed changes in the nation's public education system by leveraging the resources and vision of the private sector. NAS's founding leaders were concerned, as were the people of Chelsea and Boston University, that students were leaving school without the knowledge and skills necessary to succeed in an increasingly competitive global economy. They understood that schools had to contend with an abundance of social problems in an environment of scarce resources. New American Schools was created to develop innovative partnerships across the country dedicated to improve education opportunities for children.

While they shared a commitment to the same goal—school reform—the circumstances and approaches of New American Schools and the Boston University/Chelsea partnership couldn't have been more different. New American Schools presented a broad vision of how the private sector could support designs and programs that would break the mold and dramatically change public education. Chelsea was the effort of a single major university utilizing its resources to help improve a failing school system in its own backyard. New American Schools' "customers" were school districts and superintendents who would acquire innovative programs funded by NAS and adapt them to their own organizations completely autonomously. This agreement left NAS with little authority in how the programs were instituted.

There was also a clear political distinction. Chelsea had been a long-term Democratic voting city with strong labor relationships. New American Schools was the initiative of Republican President George H.W. Bush, which attracted supporters from his own party, and some of the largest corporations in America.

Chelsea, with its declining economy and growing immigrant population, exemplified many of the economic and demographic changes across America at the end of the 21st century. The city was also small enough to allow for looking at Chelsea's budget and being able to understand each of its accounts. Its population was small enough to know each school principal and many of the teachers, and it was possible for partnership workers to be directly in touch with the sentiments of the parents, teachers, and students. The numbers involved in Chelsea were also fairly small: $4,250 per student and a $15 million total budget for the schools. By contrast, in the early 1990s, the New American Schools' national effort had already raised over a hundred million dollars from corporate America.

Because of the ongoing discussions and controversy surrounding school funding, these numbers are important. One of John Silber's most famous contributions to this conversation compared the financing and quality of Boston and Chelsea school systems—both poor performers. He would say if you want to get an education you can pay half the price in Chelsea ($4,250 per student in 1990) for the same mediocre education that you'd pay twice as much for in Boston (approximately $8,000 per student). For Silber and many others, then as now, more money does not necessarily lead to better schooling on its own. If a school system's financial resources are not strategically and efficiently allocated, the fruits of these resources may be difficult or impossible to harvest. This point remains crucial as school districts battle for more money to improve school performance without the recognition of the underlying social and economic conditions.

By the late 1980s, the best minds in both business and education were coming to a joint recognition that the prevalent models of education reform were not working. With respect to New American Schools, corporate America understood that bold initiatives were necessary as a combined corporate effort and started allocating substantial capital to education reform.

The New American Schools initiative reveals how political education policy and praxis can be on a national level. Chelsea had proven that on a local level. By the time Democratic President Bill Clinton assumed office in 1993, the national conversation about education quality had increased substantially, and Clinton retained his Republican predecessor's New American Schools initiative to explore as many options for improving education as possible. The chairman of New American Schools at the time was David Kearns, the brilliant CEO of Xerox, who had significantly improved the company's fortunes during his tenure. David is viewed nationally as a leader in both business and education.

NEW AMERICAN SCHOOLS' FOCUS AND CHALLENGES

By 1993, the continued bipartisan support for the New American Schools initiative indicated that the program's research and development efforts were considered important by members of both political parties—a rare occurrence in education. Education research had theretofore been mostly neglected by policymakers, educators, and administrators. But from the beginning of the NAS program, Kearns, who had been keenly aware of the amount of money that businesses were spending on research and development to remain competitive, supported undertaking similar research for education. Then (and some argue, largely as now), the federal government invested virtually nothing in education research on best practices and innovative models.

The governance of New American Schools drew from top U.S. business leaders. Kearns was chairman of the board, which consisted of eighteen of the most distinguished business and education leaders in the nation, most of whom also were major donors to New American Schools. The Executive Committee included three vice-chairs: James Baker, chairman of Arvin Industries, Louis Gerstner, chairman and CEO of RJR Nabisco Corporation (later IBM Corp), and Frank Shrontz, chairman and CEO of The Boeing Company. The day-to-day direction of New American Schools was led by John L. Anderson, who served as president of New American Schools, and who had been a director of education for IBM.

The NAS environment was corporate, and major decisions were made by the executive board. The staff understood they were there, to a great extent, to vet and prepare the recommendations for the executive committee upon which the executive committee could then act upon. NAS also had an Executive Advisory Panel and a Management Advisory Council—the political equivalent of a blue ribbon panel of expert advisors. The Executive Advisory Panel was a nationwide group of outstanding educational professionals and was chaired by Saul Cooperman, a former commissioner of education in New Jersey and a national expert in education reform. There were approximately two dozen other members, including Ramon Cortines, the chancellor of New York City's Board of Education, and Peter Greer, the principal and CEO of Montclair Kimberley, as well as the former dean of the Boston University School of Education and superintendent of the Chelsea Public Schools.

Many participants in the New American Schools initiative were shocked that the private sector, so good at solving any number of business problems, was having a difficult time making progress in reforming and improving public education, even after leveraging corporate America's significant resources.

Research done by the Public Agenda Fund was of special interest. Public Agenda's polls revealed that that education was perceived, by the public at least, as the number one problem in America. But paradoxically, they found that though 90 percent of all Americans put education as their number one problem, only 10 percent said that the problem involved their child or their schools. This information only underscored the difficulty education reformers encountered in localities across America when trying to change the system.

Scalability was also heavily discussed by those involved in NAS, and it coincided with the goal of the three phases of implementation of the Design Team program. The group discussed how we would determine when a design had reached the potential and critical mass for scale. Clearly this is something not easily defined, but if the objective was to implement innovations in select jurisdictions, then they would have a better chance for success, particularly if some of these design teams had local political and education establishment connections that would result in a broader adoption of their designs in their particular geographic region.

Without ever defining exactly when scale would be reached, there was a best estimate that you needed approximately a 10–20 percent penetration rate of design acceptance in a particular region for scale; this would encourage other schools in that area to say that they too would like to have access to that particular design. NAS's difficulty in defining scale remains today. Almost twenty years later, a broadly accepted definition of "scalable" educational reform initiatives remains elusive.

Kearns drew upon his business acumen and often commented on the amount of money that the U.S. Department of Education spent on research and development (R&D), which was less than 1 percent of the DOE budget, compared to the 10–20 percent of the budget at most major U.S. technology, manufacturing, bioscience, and pharmaceutical companies. Consequently, under Kearns, New American Schools would in effect become an R&D shop for education, utilizing financial and intellectual resources from corporate America, and proving that the importance of research and development in supporting innovation and efficiency is not limited to the private sector.

SCHOOL DESIGN: REQUEST FOR PROPOSALS

NAS was also instrumental in illustrating that the desire for trying new and innovative procedures in education was not limited to the private sector. It all began in October 1991, when NAS requested proposals for new comprehensive school designs that would support higher standards and student achievement. To their great surprise, between October 1991 and July 1992,

NAS received 686 proposals from educators, community groups, and businesses in every state. Every proposal was reviewed by experienced education, business, and community leaders in a thorough evaluation process.

Only three constraints were imposed: that the design help *all* students achieve world-class standards in at least five core subjects: English, mathematics, science, history, and geography; that young people graduate prepared for responsible citizenship, further learning, and productive employment; and that, after initial investment costs, the new schools operate at costs comparable to conventional schools.

New American Schools requested these proposals because many in the private sector believed that a diversity of school designs responsive to the needs, values, interests, and capabilities of the communities they served would provide the building blocks for the best public education system possible. The common thread underlying these diverse designs was a firm set of essential principles:

* high academic standards
* strong and fair accountability and assessment measures
* curricular and instructional strategies that included thematic, project-based, and interactive learning
* continuous professional development for teachers and staff
* service to, and strong support from, parents and the community
* school autonomy and decentralized governance structures for more efficient operations
* integrated use of technology to enhance the performance of students, teachers, and schools

On July 9, 1992, eleven school Design Teams were selected to enter the first phase of a five-year, three-phased plan of action. Phase 1 was a one-year development phase to refine design concepts and implementation strategies. By June 1993, just nine of the original eleven Design Teams were selected to proceed on to Phase 2, based on their performance in Phase 1. Teams began working on site, testing their designs in diverse school settings, from rural Mississippi to inner-city Los Angeles to a Native American reservation in Minnesota. Phase 3, still to come, would be a two-year national dissemination and scale-up phase to foster systemic change through intense school implementation efforts in selected jurisdictions around the nation.

The nine teams tackled the challenge of school reform using a variety of approaches. For example, Co-NECT Schools was designed and led by Bolt, Beranek, and Newman, a world leader in communications technology. These K-12 schools were organized around small clusters of students taught by cross-disciplinary teams. They used technology to enhance every aspect of teaching, learning, professional development, and school management.

Expeditionary Learning Outward Bound drew upon the pedagogy and tradition of Outward Bound and the writings of prominent educators Eleanor Duckworth, Kurt Hahn, and Paul Ylvisaker. They used "learning expeditions"—long-term, academically rigorous interdisciplinary studies that required students to work inside and outside the classroom.

Roots and Wings was an elementary school design that built upon the widely used reading program Success for All; both were developed at the Johns Hopkins University Center for Research on Effective Schooling for Disadvantaged Students. The goal of Roots and Wings was to ensure that all children successfully graduate elementary school equipped with solid self-esteem and sound learning skills. They believed that schools must do whatever it takes to make sure all students succeed and to that end provided at-risk students with tutors, family support, and a variety of other services to meet this goal.

The balance of the original nine teams and their design focus included:

- the Audrey Cohen College System of Education: redesign the entire school setting including its curriculum to achieve meaningful purposes using a transdisciplinary approach to benefit the community and the larger world.
- Atlas Communities: steers away from fragmented, bureaucratic educational environments to create a unified, supportive community of learners. Teams of teachers work together to design curriculum and assessments based on locally defined standards. The teachers collaborate with parents and administrators to set and maintain sound management and academic policies to improve student performance.
- Community Learning Centers: contracts negotiated by the school and districts provide a structure for top-to-bottom change. Schools are held accountable for allocating resources more effectively, supporting students' high achievement. The President of Community Learning Centers, Wayne Jennings, was a founding Director of Association of Educators in Private Practice.
- Los Angeles Learning Centers: provide students with strong social support from school and community members in order to overcome the obstacles to learning faced by inner-city children. Governance and management also are restructured to engage community members in decision-making and to ensure that the design can improve and evolve. Los Angeles Learning Centers also incorporates the extensive use of advanced technology as an essential element for implementation of the design.
- The Modern Red Schoolhouse: fuse-proven, longstanding, traditional, American education principles with new instructional methods and technologies. These elements are combined with a high level of flexibility in organizing instruction and deploying resources.

- The National Alliance for Restructuring Education: redesign standards and assessments, curriculum and instruction, and management systems, creates a web of support and engages the public.

FUNDING FOR DESIGN IMPLEMENTATION

Fixing schools is not like remodeling or franchising a fast-food restaurant. Doing business with schools and school districts is different than any other sector of the economy. If you have a really good model in one school and another school nearby is failing, because of the "Balkanization" inherent to the U.S. education system, it does not necessarily mean that the underperforming school will be sufficiently aware of the existence of the better performing school down the street enough to adopt its model. To a great extent, selling to schools and implementing programs in schools is like hand-to-hand combat.

Throughout all of this, Kearns, who was also dealing with serious health issues, was able to facilitate the discussion and engage these extremely thoughtful, intelligent, and powerful executives. The amount of respect and admiration that people held for David Kearns in what could be a very contentious, political, and difficult environment was remarkable. His patience and commitment to New American Schools during challenging times was considerable.

The funding of the New American Schools initiative is also instructive. A little over $100 million had been raised between April 1991 and July 1993. Approximately half of the $100 million came from a challenge grant from the Annenberg Foundation. Additional donors included most of the nation's corporate heavyweights, such as IBM, General Motors, AT&T, Mobil, RJR Nabisco, Time Warner, and Johnson & Johnson. So in many ways, the hard work had already been done—the arms had been twisted and the "Who's Who in American Business" list responded.

While most New American Schools funders were major U.S. corporations, some had undergone recent restructuring and no longer had significant budgets to devote to education reform efforts. Much of the brainstorming thus centered around thinking about other models and methods of funding. By reaching out to some of the major technology companies in the West Coast, such as Microsoft, Cisco, and Intel, this issue of fundraising beyond the original contributors was daunting, as those involved had limited experience dealing with companies beyond their inner circle. The board was somewhat of an old boy's network. Many of the board members worked together on the Conference Board and the Business Roundtable. Some had also served on each others' company boards. They did not know of or have working relationships with many of the emerging companies in technology, software, healthcare, and bio-science. Identifying new prospects became my assignment.

Even with the money raised from the core group of top world-class companies, and their representatives in leadership roles in the organization, it was a challenge to engage them to think creatively about new markets and scale issues. The corporate affairs officer's major responsibility in stewarding their company's donation to New American Schools was influenced by the lens of how the corporate leader was viewed externally. While helping the kids was a priority, it was often second to the agenda of the company and its public relations image.

Both the Walton Family Foundation and the Annenberg Foundation, both established by two great business leaders of that time, Sam Walton of Wal-Mart and Walter Annenberg of Triangle Publications, were strong supporters of the initiative. These entrepreneurs had the foresight to move their resources from a corporate foundation to an independent foundation that did not have the same concerns in keeping a CEO in a positive light. This period was before the enormous wealth creation that enabled entrepreneurs such as Bill Gates, Eli Broad, and Donald Fisher (referred to frequently in this book) to create their own foundations, which most often focused on education.

RESULTS OF NEW AMERICAN SCHOOLS

Ultimately, the New American Schools initiative proved a significant contrast to the work in Chelsea. In Chelsea, the unifying goal was helping kids in a poor and impoverished city and, in many ways, was "easier" than achieving the goals of NAS because of its focus and vision within one community. Though the Boston University/Chelsea partnership had to navigate among certain diverse groups to build consensus, dealing with one city is much easier than trying to build consensus on a national or even regional level. The politics between Boston University and Chelsea leaders seldom affected our fundraising to the extent the national level politics did with New American Schools.

In addition to the different political challenges, the other significant difference between the Chelsea effort and the more ambitious program goals of New American Schools was, as often happens in politics, about control and the management process. If NAS was to be accountable for outcomes, who managed the oversight of the design teams who contracted with the school districts? In Chelsea there was a great deal of oversight with regard to Boston University's management and performance—the School Committee. These issues regarding oversight of the design team were the responsibility of the NAS leadership—but NAS lacked oversight or the equivalent of a "school committee" to ask the hard questions about success and outcomes. This was a concern of donors, and it was clear that management was keenly aware and focused on the issue of oversight.

NAS's inability to find methods and strategies to recoup its investment in the design models was also thorny and not easily resolvable. At this point, charter school legislation and for-profit school systems were still in their infancy. NAS was the first major effort of its type to pave the way for others. It truly was an experiment, but at least it was an innovative attempt to affect, a resourceful model for education reform.

NAS illustrated how important research was going to be to the growing education reform movement, and the initiative's existence planted the seeds for what eventually became EduVentures, a research firm to support the emerging education industry. NAS undertook broad and commendable vision to improve research and design in education. Unfortunately, Phase 3 of the design and implementation efforts to reach scale was not accomplished. There is a fundamental limitation to how much impact a top-down, corporate-driven initiative from the outside can ultimately have in fostering true reform in education, since control and accountability reside at the school or district level.

So, was it was worth raising over $100 million for a program that in the short-term did not succeed in transforming education?

Yes.

As with the Boston University/Chelsea agreement, which was drawn up initially for ten years, and subsequently renewed for another seven, education reform is measured in terms of decades, not years. We are still in the midst of an education reform effort that has yet to mature and bear the desired fruit, and NAS was a critical component of our progress thus far. It explicitly invited the business community to take a stake in the nation's education system.

The substance of *A Nation At Risk's* goals, emphasizing accountability and performance, became a priority for the efforts of all the NAS Design Teams. Ultimately the efforts in support of greater accountability led to the passage of the "No Child Left Behind" legislation, which has its own advocates and detractors. The New American Schools put the question of how to scale education reform questions firmly in the forefront of political discussions and resulted in an ongoing, greater discussion about national benchmarking, standards, and accountability.

The New American Schools effort did not transform education, but it did help prioritize the agenda and laid the groundwork for future entrepreneurs. New American Schools brought together thousands of business leaders, educators, political leaders, and teachers to become part of a grand transformative effort. Many of those individuals, whether business people, entrepreneurs or educators, were inspired and went from that challenge to pursue endeavors of their own as successful education entrepreneurs in enterprises they created.

While New American Schools clearly had a public relations benefits for the companies involved, it also genuinely fostered public engagement in the business of education reform. This began with the 686 applications for Design Teams. Clearly, many in America felt they could participate in the change process. Once the final Design Teams were selected, there were significant collaborations between some of the nation's most committed and experienced school administrators, policy makers, teachers, and other business leaders. Many of these same people went on to work in other experiments in school reform and have later mentioned that the vision cast by New American Schools was their motivator.

In addition to its public relations and public engagement legacies, New American Schools also encouraged private philanthropy in the area of education reform and in promoting what would become one of the most far-reaching reform efforts, the charter school movement. In the 1990s, a new group of successful entrepreneurs began to emerge who wanted to give back the same way that corporate leaders did when they supported New American Schools. It was the emergence of the charter school movement that provided local, and somewhat less ambitious but equally important, avenues for donors to participate in education reform. Sponsoring, adopting, and funding schools has become an important, socially responsible topic, and business friends and their spouses became committed and knowledgeable about the issues. Some of the most compelling efforts were those made by major foundations to support the new charter schools. In 2009, in Los Angeles alone, six foundations now support 170 charter schools. Many of the leaders in this work participated in some way in the New American Schools effort.

David Kearns, in particular, serves as a model for what is possible in educational entrepreneurship. Regarded as one of the most respected business leaders in America, he had achieved international acclaim for the turnaround job he did at Xerox. He used that acclaim to its most effective potential through his wide activity in business and philanthropic organizations, such as the Business Roundtable, the Ford Foundation, and the Urban League. When President Bush called him and asked him to serve as deputy secretary of education under Secretary of Education Lamar Alexander, he accepted, even though he was not the top dog. For David, title was never as important as challenge, opportunity, and the ability to concretely make a difference.

Kearns lived his commitment to education and to the people he worked with on a daily basis. When he traveled to raise funds for NAS, he made it a point to greet each person he encountered by name and on the way out say goodbye to them by name. His interest in people was genuine, and he would have been an incredible, authentic politician. One of the more interesting trips we made together was a fundraising visit and Design Team site visit in Los Angeles. One of our appointments was with Michael Milken, who had recently returned to his office after spending some time in prison for his conviction related to insider trading. Michael had been diagnosed with prostate cancer in his examination before leaving prison. Some of the people from NAS were a little uneasy about the public relations ramifications of David meeting with Michael, but David was certainly not. During this meeting it was interesting to learn that Michael had used David's book, *Winning the Brain Race,* to teach competitiveness to inmates while he was in prison. Another example of Kearns' lifelong commitment to learning and education without judgment.

By the end of 1993, Kearns had accepted an appointment at Harvard Business School and Harvard's Graduate School of Education. He was going there to teach and research organizational change, at which he had become an expert through his experiences at Xerox, the U.S. Department of Education, and New American Schools, as well being an author of books on this topic. This serendipitous move meant that Boston now had Kearns as a local resource. The time was ripe to build an enterprise, as well as help build the fledgling education industry.

Chapter 4

Venturing into Education

Chapter 4 shows the challenges and successes of the early stages of establishing a business venture as an education entrepreneur. Long before "social entrepreneurship" became trendy, education entrepreneurs were taking private resources and applying them to creating public good in the education sector. This chapter provides lessons for the reader to consider when forming their own business. It chronicles the period in the 1990s when the term "education industry" was coined and illustrates the distinct sectors of early education companies. These sectors (providing services, selling products, or operating schools within the education market) provided the foundation of today's education industry. The chapter illustrates when the education industry first became diversified beyond bricks and mortar initiatives and marks an evolution representing new companies founded by entrepreneurs.

By the early 1990s, it was becoming clear that technology would serve as the driver behind the next phase of education reform. The experiences at Harvard, Chelsea, and then with New American Schools made plain that the greatest opportunities for education reform would be created by entrepreneurs. It had taken John Silber, an entrepreneur, to conceive, plan, and execute the Boston University/Chelsea school partnership. Through New American Schools, corporate America proved that it was prepared to help in the education-reform movement; they do, of course, have a self interest in doing so because of their needs for a better educated and trained workforce. Nevertheless, there are few CEOs willing to make the commitment that David Kearns did when he left Xerox at the top of his game to serve his country.

Creating the company, EduVentures, made sense because of the Harvard, Chelsea, and New American School experiences, the evolution of the education market, and a gap of research and information. By 1993, it had become clear that private-sector companies could provide products and services to improve educational opportunities for children—and further still, that a market for such goods was starting to grow strongly. EduVentures would support "Private Ventures for the Public Good" (the company motto), but would differ greatly from the other growing education market segment: for-profit school management business. In 1993, the for-profit school management business was too political, too local, and, frankly, too risky!

The experience at NAS also clarified the potential impact and future opportunities in education for entrepreneurs. NAS attracted the best and brightest talent that business and education had to offer. Education entrepreneurs committed to education reform tend to be better suited to make a long commitment as it is their sole career focus and drive. In addition, entrepreneurs can also withstand the political pressures better than corporate America, which is often forced to avoid conflict. Corporate America was also stymied by their responsibility to their company's mission and responsibility to their shareholders.

Because of my distribution experience and understanding of this role in an industry, EduVentures would focus on serving the role of the "middleman" to other education industry providers and producers, a niche that seemed to fit a need in the industry in this early stage. EduVentures was established to serve the education market as a distributor of information and as friend of other education-sector entrepreneurs who sought capital. The company responded to the market's need to define itself (still unclear in the early 1990s), engage the financial and investment community to understand that education was a viable industry ripe for attention, and established a niche to bring the two groups (entrepreneurs and investors) together.

CEOs, including Rick Holden of the J.L Hammett School Supplies Company, The Learning Company's Michael Perik, Tom Snyder of Tom Snyder Production, and the founders of Bright Horizon Childcare Company, Roger Brown and Linda Mason, all agreed the market was ripe for expansion and capital infusions and was in great need of market research and high quality information. EduVentures' potential success as a business hinged on where the roles of friend of the entrepreneur and champion of the industry intersected.

THE BEGINNING

EduVentures became a legal entity in December of 1993, when it was still in its earliest stages of development. It was clear that making a difference and contributing to the ongoing process of education reform was going to take years, even in the private sector. "Think in decades," said David Kearns, who served as the first investor of the new company. EduVentures was founded to utilize private resources to create public good and private gain. The company would benefit its own investors, facilitate the growth of the education market, and ultimately, help some of the thousands of students who wind their way through the U.S. education system every year.

In the early stages of developing EduVentures, it was important to research and outline the emerging education industry, which at the time was still in its nascent phase. This research served to define the competitive landscape and establish a more formal plan for the company. The plan was to be one that would clearly stand the test of time, be scalable and profitable, and by extension, benefit children and schools.

A three-legged stool provided the appropriate model for EduVentures' structure in its early days. The first, quality research and independent information, served to simultaneously build an industry and a company; the second, a trade association and advocacy group of like minded people, would create a network of customers for EduVentures and support the growing industry; and the third, developing future education industry leaders at the graduate-school level who would create a new generation of education entrepreneurs. For the business to succeed in the education market, it needed all three legs of the stool to find firm footing; if it was missing one of the legs, the stool would not be able to stand.

In retrospect, the concept of the three legs holding up the stool also served as a model for the foundation for the growth of a new industry, as well as the foundation for EduVentures and an education industry. The first leg of the stool was to build a highly trusted independent source of research and information for the market. The ability to advise and attract entrepreneurs with scalable businesses would be the by-product of the credibility created by the information. In addition, this research would demonstrate to the investment community and other stakeholders that the education industry could be profitable in the private sector, while doing "good" for the public.

The next leg was to bring together like-minded people to share ideas and experiences and have an association to advocate their point of view. The vision resulted in my involvement with Chris Yelich and the Association of Educators in Private Practice (AEPP). Entrepreneurs needed soul mates to share ideas and experiences, and this Association provided that outlet. Such an industry association was needed to serve as the voice for all sectors of the market, and in 2002, AEPP became the Education Industry Association (EIA).

The third leg of the stool was important for the future leaders in the industry, who could come from graduate schools of either business or education (or both). Then, as now, there was a tremendous lack of understanding and trust between the two groups, creating a knowledge gap that, when bridged, can serve to build capacity and improve outcomes for a broad audience. The business students' perception was that education was failing, and the fault lay with the education schools and poorly trained teachers. The education students felt the business school students were totally insensitive to the hard and important work of teachers, educators, and administrators and were only interested in finding fault and, of course, opportunities for making money. There were, however, many graduate students who had a real interest in both business and education, and some of these students later served as the entrepreneurs who have made an impact on the education industry in the past twenty years.

This third leg, while it did not yield any short-term profits, was critical in developing a permanent foundation for the future leadership of the education industry. It also served as an excellent recruiting tool for the building of EduVentures and as a reference and resource for our clients.

THE FORMATIVE YEARS

Many of the leaders of the education industry today got their start at the same time as EduVentures' formative years. Today, they are leading organizations such as Teach for America, the NewSchools Venture Fund, the KIPP Academies, and numerous for-profit ventures such as Knowledge Universe, Sylvan Learning Centers, Kaplan Education, Bright Horizons Family Solutions, National Heritage Academies, and Edison Schools. Because of the nascent stage of the education industry at this point, EduVentures was serving somewhat as a "hub" for entrepreneurs and education industry people who would otherwise have been operating solo. Many of today's successful entrepreneurs in education established their companies in the early 1990s, and whether through EduVentures activities or the Education Industry Association and its predecessors—Association of Educators in Private Practice—they became close colleagues.

One of those entrepreneurs who stands out as a symbol of the good things to come for education was Wendy Kopp, who founded Teach For America in 1987, after graduating from Princeton University. Wendy had a plan to allow college graduates without an education degree to work and assist in the K-12 schools. The results have been outstanding, and one key reason is because she and her original team are still committed to and involved in the organization.

EduVentures' motto, "Private Ventures for the Public Good," expressed the belief that the private sector could have a significant role in improving the lot in life of, and opportunities for, children. If public education is viewed as a monopoly, bringing competition into the "marketplace" would inspire improvement in education, subsequently improving the lives of America's schoolchildren and expanding their future opportunities. Why could the private sector not improve opportunities for the kids and markets at the same time? Unfortunately, this view of market competition in education was not always greeted with open arms.

As a practical matter, direct confrontations with school administrations or teachers' unions rarely bear fruit. In the union's view, private companies managing schools or school districts also seemed questionably efficient, at best. Having witnessed this first hand through the battles between Boston University and the teachers' union in Chelsea, interventions by outsiders were often invitations for public controversy and political battles. Politically, education is a state and local issue and an emotional and political hot button for many diverse public constituencies. But the oft-suggested move by some political conservatives that we abolish the U.S. Department of Education seems drastic and unnecessary. The Department of Education's best role is to serve as a bully pulpit rather than determining and enforcing national education policy.

The private sector also offered the possibility of bringing new technologies into the classroom, which some felt would be the key drivers of change-enhancing student performance. This was an opportunity for business, since the public was beginning to realize the benefits of having technology in the classroom. At New American Schools, a key issue was "public engagement" for school improvement. Many of the organization's leaders, particularly Lou Gerstner of IBM, saw technology as the agent to create "public engagement." There seemed to be much business potential for infusing education with new tools and techniques that would enhance student learning and scale would be created.

Aware of these challenges, EduVentures submotto was, "To Supplement, Not to Supplant," to make private sector activities non-threatening and not be viewed as a corporate takeover of schools. We positioned the education industry as enriching the public schools. Lamar Alexander often referred to the education industry as a "niche" industry. Consequently, from the beginning, EduVentures was primarily focused on the companies that supported education providers, such as supplemental publishers, tutoring, test preparation, after-school programs, distance learning, and software and educational products. These companies took the political process out of the equation because they were considered supportive and less invasive of the existing structure.

In beginning to explore the "private ventures" part of EduVentures, it was clear there were a significant number of entrepreneurs who were interested in establishing businesses to improve education opportunities. They needed help creating business plans and raising capital, and, like typical entrepreneurs, were in a rush for EduVentures to "support, implement, and execute" bringing their ideas to market.

But at this point, EduVentures still needed to hone in on defining the market and its needs. More data needed to be gathered. So EduVentures worked to size the market and define each of its logical sectors. At the time those included schools (K-12 and post-secondary), corporate training, and product and service companies. Concrete, tangible data was needed that would withstand any scrutiny to gain credibility for the EduVentures brand.

In the spring of 1994, Joe Wagner, a Wharton MBA student, who was specifically interested in the education space and was an analytical, quantitative thinker, came knocking and helped to identify businesses in different sectors, such as early childhood and after-school programs, educational software, publishing, and school supplies. We researched every business we could find that had a direct link to the education market. We described each business and then refined the data on their particular sector. What ultimately developed was the first Education Industry Directory. This directory would prove to be the precursor to the kind of research for which EduVentures would begin to be known. In a way, the Directory and its data became the gold standard for those seeking to understand the emerging education industry. Eventually, Joe went on to form a chain of for-profit private schools in California that was sold to a venture capital/private equity group for several million dollars eight years after its inception.

In the beginning, a source of revenue was to seek out and identify, from the directory of contacts, companies and ideas for the investment community. One of EduVentures' first consulting projects was in early 1994 for the owners of Geneve Corporation. Geneve was a substantial family insurance business with a keen interest in and a commitment to education. EduVentures researched the market and opportunities for acquisitions and developed a strategy for scaling NASCO, a major school supply businesses that they had recently acquired. Geneve has built a series of successful and profitable education companies, demonstrating again that one of the keys to succeeding in the education market is undying passion for education and a steadfast commitment to slow and steady growth over the long run. Their holdings today are consolidated in a publicly held company appropriately called Aristotle Corporation.

In early 1994, EduVentures consulted for Jon Carson's Family Education Network by identifying potential strategic partners. The Family Education Network provided important information to connect parents, teachers, and school administrators through newsletters and, ultimately, online communication. The information could be as simple as a task of notifying parents of the school menu, upcoming special events at the school, or important policy issues. It became the preferred link between parents and teachers at many schools and was recognized by the national Parent Teachers Association. The business was sold to Pearson Education in the heyday of the dot-com era (1999) for $126 million.

The company also worked closely with Sherry Speakman, who was responsible for Coopers & Lybrand's K-12 efforts. Coopers & Lybrand had built an international reputation as the leading accounting and consulting firm supporting American higher education institutions. Gene Freedman, the chairman of Coopers, wanted to focus on ways in which Coopers & Lybrand could utilize its resources to help America's biggest education challenge, which he identified not as higher education, but K-12. Coopers & Lybrand realized that it would take many years to recoup a major investment, as it was nearly impossible for a business consulting firm to wrap itself around a short-term remedy for the many K-12 issues. Gene introduced Sherry Speakman, who was a very successful mergers and acquisitions consultant for the firm. Sherry was asked by the company to build the foundation for their K-12 practice.

One of Sherry's first assignments was to try to solve a major political battle in New York City. There, the mayor, the chancellor of schools, and the controller were engaged in a highly profiled debate over a major shortfall of the New York Public School budget. The amount of money at stake was in the hundreds of millions of dollars, as the total budget from New York's public schools at that time was in the range of $5 billion (versus $15 billion today). Sherry met with the involved parties and volunteered to try to wrap herself around the budgetary crisis.

In addition to authorizing Sherry's time, Coopers also provided six additional consultants on a pro bono basis. They began to organize and retrieve information on the schools' finances and accounting models. It was hard to believe but there were no accurate censuses of the schools and their assets. From a reporting basis, there was no consistent financial chart of accounts for analysis and comparison. In many circumstances, school names and buildings popped up that New York school officials didn't even know existed. After many months of research and effort, Sherry developed a new, comprehensive chart of accounts that was clear and applicable to all New York City schools.

Despite the importance of this work, there was limited interest from other districts in replicating it. Nevertheless, Sherry pursued this work in her own company as an independent consultant. She provided consulting projects leads to EduVentures and vice-versa. Working with Sherry provided EduVentures a look at the day-to-day operations of individual schools and underscored the belief that schools don't necessarily need *more* money—they need better management of it. Once you become a believer in true education reform, it is very difficult to walk away! Sherry proved to be another example of the kind of person who succeeds in this arena—one who has the passion to be in it for the long haul and to not be swayed by rejection and bureaucracy.

Another entrepreneur entering the industry in the 1990s was Michael Milken. Michael's vision was broad and clear. He, too, saw technology as a driver for educational progress. His company, Knowledge Universe, was originally called Education Technology. Today, Knowledge Universe is the largest private investment fund in education. Michael also built a very important philanthropic arm with his brother Lowell called The Milken Family Foundation. Over twenty years, the Milken Family Foundation has given tens of millions of dollars to teachers for technology innovation in the classroom. Complementing these two efforts in a three-legged stool of their own, is the Milken Research Institute. In less than ten years, the Milken Institute has become a leading public policy voice on economic growth, job creation, and capital formation.

EXPANSION

During these early days of EduVentures, the company needed a controllable payroll and minimal overhead. Its first full-time hire, Jessica Lee, came from A Different September Foundation. After ADSF, Jessica had gone on to get her MBA at Boston University and wanted to pursue her interest in the for-profit education market. The company later hired Arthur Steinert, who had developed education software products prior to becoming a teacher. Arthur joined EduVentures as a consultant until he departed for the University of Pennsylvania's Wharton School to pursue his MBA. Arthur helped build EduVentures' consulting practice and, through his efforts, increased our revenues by three-fold in our second year of operation in 1996 to 1997. He knew the power of technology from his own practical experience and was an effective consultant with strong analytical skills. After completing Wharton, Arthur returned to help execute its new business model, just as EduVentures was ready to expand its research offerings with a syndicated subscription model.

In the spring of 1995, Jon Carson, of Family Education Network, arranged an introduction to John McLaughlin. John was originally from Alabama and had moved with his family to Minnesota. He possessed a pleasant smile and had a charming southern drawl. He had a pedigree in education, including degrees from Vanderbilt and the University of Chicago. John's involvement with the education industry began with the establishment of a private alternative school in Nashville called Benton Hall School, which dealt with special education students with learning disabilities. John also was a tenured professor of education at Vanderbilt.

Once he established the Benton Hall School, he began to see a market opportunity for alternative education. He decided that rather than operate schools himself, he would venture into the newsletter business and established the *Education Investor,* which he coyly said he wrote part-time in the basement of his home. He had modest means, but possessed a very curious and analytical mind and was a gifted writer. He was able to describe and understand education issues quickly and had an eye for seeing value.

The *Education Investor* focused on investments and transactions by public and private sector companies in education and also included commentaries from outside experts and CEOs. While its subscription list was small, it was distinguished and included some of the most highly regarded operators and opinion leaders in the education market. Many of those subscribers went on to become the most successful entrepreneurs in the education industry, including Chris Whittle at Edison, John Sperling at Apollo, and Doug Becker at Sylvan Learning.

After the introduction, EduVentures assessed the opportunity of having a separate newsletter become part of its business. The meeting about the acquisition of *Education Investor* was the first official circumstance where "The Education Industry" was identified as such. Once EduVentures acquired the newsletter, the name changed from *Education Investor* to *The Education Industry Report.* Consequently, it seemed that on April 30, 1995, the "Education Industry" was officially born.

The April meeting in 1995 resulted in a handshake agreement that EduVentures would acquire controlling interest in the *Education Investor.* The assets would include the intellectual property, including all research and consulting reports, historical data, the *Education Investor* subscription list, and the execution of an employment and non-compete agreement with John. We realized we were in the process of establishing a "language" for the industry. The new business would be a separate entity from EduVentures. It was agreed that EduVentures would be the consulting and financial advisory firm, and *The Education Industry Report* would be a subscription-based newsletter with news and commentary on the emerging education market. Geographic distance and company missions would distinguish the two companies.

At the time, the *Education Investor* was very well written and had excellent financial information on the performance and the transactions of all the publicly held education companies during the period between 1992 and 1995. Some of the companies covered closely in the newsletter were Education Alternatives, Education Development Corporation, DeVry, Education Publishing Group, Children's Comprehensive Services, Children's Discovery, The Learning

Company, Sylvan Learning System, and Bright Ideas. In the 1990s, it seemed apparent that education could become a $100 billion industry over time. In 1995, it was approximately $50 billion. John maintained an opinion column in *The Education Industry Report,* focusing on the trends and the future direction of the education industry. His column became a must read for industry leaders.

John also wrote many interesting and important commentaries and in-depth interviews with policy leaders and heads of teachers' unions, the American Federation of Teachers and the National Education Association. The head of the National School Board Association served on the *Education Investor* advisory board. John also wrote an outstanding essay making the case for the existance of an education industry that has stood the test of time.

EduVentures acquired control (50.1 percent) of the *Education Investor* in June 1995, three months after the original meeting in Boston. The *Education Investor* was officially re-launched as *The Education Industry Report* in September 1995, bumping subscriptions from 79 to 250. A major direct mailing saw less than a 1 percent return on the mailing, perhaps because the price increased from $79 to $199. These lukewarm results served as a warning sign that even a nominally priced newsletter did not possess a large demand. While there was a lot of interest in the for-profit education market, people were reluctant to spend money to learn more about investment opportunities and the marketplace. Nonetheless, the newsletter reached the major decision-makers in the industry.

THE POWER OF MARKET RESEARCH

By the beginning of fall 1995, work on The Education Industry Directory had been completed. The introduction defined the overall market for education at $600 billion or 9 percent of GDP. It was a defining moment for EduVentures and for the industry as a whole. The market size was clearly defined, as we had all of the numbers cross-referenced between our own internal data and numbers from other outside research companies. The data produced had never been seen before by the education or investment community in this format. The directory was sold for $199, but often it was free to subscribers of the newsletter.

Relatively speaking, the Directory generated modest financial success, but enormous publicity. It was first distributed in November and December of 1995. On January 31, 1996, the report and its findings made the front page of *The New York Times* "above the fold." It read like a Who's Who of the education and academic community, covering the education market. This public relations coup paid off significantly. From that point forward, EduVentures never had to market or solicit consulting or financial advisory activity.

The article in the *New York Times* referred to the launch of the first education industry conference for the education companies and institutional investors, hosted by Lehman Brothers. EduVentures had done previous research work with Lehman Brothers, a company that had a strong interest in education. They had built a substantial practice in healthcare and saw great potential and similarity in education. Two of their top partners, Mary Tanner and Fred Frank (husband and wife), moved from the healthcare group to help establish their education practice. In addition, they hired a highly regarded industry analyst, Michael Moe, to lead the research efforts in education. EduVentures helped plan the first two conferences in the education industry with Lehman and highlighted some of the original education industry trailblazers. Michael Moe's original investment thesis and market definition coupled with EduVentures' research was an accelerator that benefited both of us.

The first of the two major conferences hosted by Lehman Brothers took place in February 1996. Mary Tanner co-organized the conference with Michael Moe. Without a doubt, the two of them had pulled off a major coup and established an advantage from an investment bank perspective by being the first movers in the education industry. Michael Moe went on to be regarded as one of the foremost authorities in the investment community on the education market. He ultimately expanded his company into other sectors of the economy under the company name ThinkEquity and later sold his company, in 2007, to an international investment conglomerate. In late 2008 Michael launched his newest venture, Next Up!, which is a group of economic- and investment-oriented online newsletters. The newsletters cover what he refers to as "the next economy" that includes timely information on the knowledge and social learning markets.

Some of the companies present at the Lehman Brothers' conference were ITT Education, TRO, The Edison Project, Kinder Care Learning, The Apollo Group, Discovery Centers, Davidson and Associates, 10th Planet, DeVry, Learning Tree, University Online, Alternative Public Schools, and Corporate Family Solutions. Each of these companies was either publicly held or private but considering going public. They all possessed well-defined business models, and the sectors that they served included higher education, K-12 school management, alternative education, and special needs. They were all clearly the market leaders. There was no question that the investment community attending the meeting felt that they had just seen the best and brightest in the education industry and that the industry was full of opportunity and potential.

EduVentures received several consulting projects from conference participants and from other clients who read the *New York Times* article. It needed to expand staff, and so hired two additional consultants with experience in the investment community—Mark Watkins, an analyst from Smith

Barney, and Julie Horowitz, who recently had graduated from Yale University's School of Management.

FUTURE GROWTH OPPORTUNITIES

EduVentures' future could have taken one of many directions, from becoming an investment bank to establishing itself as a private investment and venture fund, or operating as a market research and consulting and advisory firm. Staff acquisitions reflected these possibilities, as the company needed to maintain flexibility for future growth.

EduVentures strategic advisory role and new business development work was aligned with the possibility of creating an education fund. Often, client selection was based on prospects for a future investment in the company. The same criteria applied to the issue of merger and acquisition support, where we sought companies where there was the possibility for investment at a later date. With these objectives on the investment side, EduVentures began to develop a proprietary database of companies, hoping to be recognized as the headquarters for "deal flow."

EduVentures itself was growing dramatically at that time and required additional staff, but we could not really grow to scale selling newsletters at $299. The business model had to be rethought to achieve a more scalable business. Unarguably, EduVentures was a business with substantial market interest and demand. As an industry founder, we had first-to-move advantage, as well as a competitive advantage in public relations and communications. The media contacted us first to verify numbers as to the size of the market; the phone was ringing on a daily basis for people not only requesting information but services for fees. Gene Freedman, chairman of Coopers & Lybrand, outlined EduVentures' challenge: "You are sitting on a gold mine . . . all you have to do is figure out how to mine the gold." There was no easy or short-term solution to this challenge.

When EduVentures acquired *Education Investor*, it was important to develop a truly functioning advisory board. It was important that John McLaughlin gain credibility as a spokesman for the education industry. The Advisory Board included David Kearns and John Dunlop, as well as Jeannie Allen, founder of the Center for Education Reform, who was a key leader of the charter school movement. Others on the board were Bill Ballard, CEO of Children's Comprehensive Services, a substantial publicly held company in the special education market; Denis Doyle, a highly regarded senior officer in the U.S. Department of Education and a Senior Fellow in Education at the Heritage Foundation; Gib Hentschke, dean of the School of Education at the University of Southern California; Harold Seamon, deputy executive director of the National School Boards Association; Bill Walton, president of Education Partners; Chris Yelich, an active board member who was founding director of Association Educators in Private Practice; and Michael Moe, vice president of Lehman Brothers.

These folks added tremendous credibility to *The Education Industry Report* and EduVentures. EduVentures had its own advisory board, but the real objective was to help shape the influence and potential for *The Education Industry Report* as the voice of the industry. Doing so would provide the opportunity for EduVentures to be viewed as the leading authority on the market. From a self-interested point of view, EduVentures was given first look at any potential advisory and consulting work. In many ways it was a no-lose situation.

The honeymoon was short-lived, however, as it soon became clear that dividing involvement between these dual enterprises was not going to work. It was essential to understand the difference in psyche and mindset between a private-sector entrepreneur and an education entrepreneur coming from academia, which was John's background. It is very difficult to be a market leader, industry innovator, and champion of the entrepreneur, while building a sustainable financial model. EduVentures would do advisory and consulting work that would allow scaling up in the future.

Most of EduVentures employees were people who understood both sides of the street, people with backgrounds in education and in business. Those who had MBAs or Masters in Education and former teachers were the most appealing candidates. EduVentures wanted to build an organization of people who would be able to put themselves in the shoes of teachers, while also being business savvy and able to identify business opportunities.

In May 1996, EduVentures organized a conference at the Kennedy School of Government with the title "Business Opportunities in Education." The experience with this event illustrates the ongoing tensions between the business and education communities. The day before the conference, the Office of the Dean of Harvard's Graduate School of Education, called to say the dean was getting a lot of negative feedback from his faculty and students. These individuals were upset with the fact that some key faculty members were participating in a conference in which children were being treated like "pawns for business," as indicated by its title "Business Opportunities in Education." While the conversation was collegial, the dean implied that even though it was last minute, we should consider canceling the conference. The conference went ahead as scheduled.

The conference was sponsored by the Kennedy School's Center for Business and Government and its director, Roger Porter. Roger had returned to the

Kennedy School after a distinguished career in government, which included his most recent stint as special advisor to President George H. W. Bush on domestic policy; clearly, there was a high priority on education.

Roger was pleased to support the Conference even though he knew the title of the event "Business Opportunities in Education" would be controversial. In fact, after the event he wrote a brief note saying that the panel was a success and that in his view, "It was largely successful because of the quality of the panelists and the audience." He felt that both were extremely sophisticated and that this was precisely the kind of activity that the Center for Business and Government should foster and encourage.

The event was held in the afternoon and after a brief welcome from Roger there was a panel discussion moderated by John McLaughlin. EduVentures' role was to do the closing by engaging the audience in a discussion about their interpretation of the opportunities in the education industry. It was a classic private venture/public good discussion. The role of John McLaughlin serving as the moderator was perfect, as he was positioned as a seasoned academic and the expert in the for-profit market. The other panelists were Roger Brown, CEO of Bright Horizons Children's Centers; Michael Perik, CEO of Soft Key International, which ultimately became the Learning Company; Bill Bowman, president of Logal Software; and Chris Whittle, president and CEO of the Edison Project.

The event at the Kennedy School was televised on C-SPAN, and while the audience was limited, the conference certainly had positioned *The Education Industry Report* and EduVentures as the industry experts. Before the advent of YouTube, C-SPAN was one way to get information out into the ether. Imagine the benefit of C-SPAN televising such an event in 1996. There was a sense that the event was historic.

After the conference, some of John's new employees were discussing the possibility that *The Education Industry Report* could do the same consulting work for them that EduVentures provided for some of the attendees. To be competitive, they would probably try to do so most likely at a lower price. This was the red flag that ultimately resulted in realizing that the arrangement between *The Education Industry Report* and EduVentures could not be sustained over the long term. It was understood from the beginning that the relationship would be one of economic control by EduVentures, and that the roles and relationships were supposed to be separated by a Chinese wall as related to research on the industry and consulting. Unfortunately, by the end of 1996, it was clear that the business marriage of *The Education Industry Report* and EduVentures needed to end. This outcome would result in a financial loss but was necessary to try to reach a win-win strategy.

Seven months after we began our partnership, I sold back my controlling interest in *The Education Industry Report* to John. Unfortunately, the only money I was able to recoup was enough to give David Kearns his investment back with a modest return, but this was done with a better understanding of the distinction and expectations between an entrepreneur from academia and an entrepreneur from business who had many a for-profit company.

AN IMPORTANT LESSON

For any change agent, any innovator, any entrepreneur, any good leader, every moment is a teachable moment and learning experience. This experience taught that high-quality data creates value; that publicity plays a huge role in launching a new business—and a new industry; and that operating for the public good in a for-profit environment is a huge financial challenge

What was made most clear is how fortunate Americans are to have grown up in the United States. This country is constantly, and ever more quickly, changing. The flow of and access to information makes learning more immediate. And so it is with the impulse to make schools better for our kids. It takes many forms and finds many channels, but the passionate young educator, the young policy wonk, and the young elected official will see the opportunity to continue to improve.

Chapter 5

The Journey and Challenges of Scale and Profitability

Chapter 5 highlights the entry of the investment community into the education sector. This evolution was important, as it validated the efforts of early entrepreneur. It also serves to show a glimpse of the energy circulating at the time, and the importance of the networking and the exchange of innovative ideas that was going on between education entrepreneurs at the time. This chapter begins to define the issues and challenges of creating a scalable enterprise in education.

For whatever reason, the change of ownership, a separation of roles, or the direct competition with *The Education Industry Report* for consulting was the exact catalyst EduVentures needed to proceed to its next phase. Selling *The Education Industry Report* was an important learning experience. I learned that as entrepreneurs we thrive on competition. It was evident that EduVentures needed to build its own brand and team—and it was well positioned to do so. The value and importance of the information and research it was generating was significant. We aimed to make the EduVentures brand and quality of work our competitive advantage.

EduVentures avoided entangling itself in the complex and controversial policy issues such as school choice, school vouchers, and for-profit school management. In the long run, policy changes might create space for more market-based opportunities in education, but EduVentures felt better served pursuing opportunities that could improve education more immediately. There were plenty of market opportunities in other arenas besides the hot button political issues.

Boston served as EduVentures' home base. Often described as the "Athens of America," Boston is home to some of the finest colleges and universities in the world. Many of them have created and produced important research and new innovations in education. Boston is also a center for investment and venture capital. Where better to focus efforts on building an education industry company? Boston was an ideal environment in which to learn about some of the most exciting new education companies and to identify prospective clients. It was also the home to almost one hundred supplementary education companies, including Houghton Mifflin Company, the largest publisher in the K-12 market in the United States.

THE POWER OF BUSINESS NETWORKING

In late 1996, Nader Dareshori, the CEO of Houghton Mifflin, had agreed to host a meeting of local Boston education companies. The purpose of the meeting was to bring together budding entrepreneurs with innovative education enterprises, in both service and product companies in the Boston area, to share ideas and experiences. It was a very wise choice by Nader for himself and his shareholders.

As a highly respected education entrepreneur, Nader's extraordinary career moves would include his eventual sale of Houghton Mifflin to the Vivendi Corporation. Only a few years later, he would sell a private investment firm he had established named Cambium Partners to Veronis Suhler Stevenson in a transaction valued at approximately $200 million dollars.

The meeting with Nader was such a success that he assigned his senior vice president, Liz Hacking, to work with me and help organize the gathering. I invited fellow education entrepreneurs who I sensed were ready and willing to become part of a peer group. We called the group the Greater Boston Education Industry Council (GBEIC). The GBEIC was the first organization of its type in the education industry. The membership was open and the council consisted of leading education companies in the greater Boston area. The original database included presidents, CEOs, and other key executives of approximately eighty education industry companies that represented every sector of the market.

The purpose of the meetings was to have member companies present their businesses to other members and to share their knowledge of the market. Those who criticize business as being merely about competition usually fail to understand the importance of collegiality and knowledge sharing in promoting successful market activity, particularly in an emerging industry.

The meetings were held bimonthly and the presenters were all local members of Boston companies. Houghton Mifflin provided meeting space in their board room, and the GBEIC had so much talent in the membership that there was very little need for outside speakers. The discussion at our first meeting in April 1997 focused on the Internet and its role in the education industry. At that meeting, participants from Bolt, Beranek, and Newman (widely credited with founding the Internet) presented potential Internet applications for education. While the programs ran for an hour and a half, the group members tended to linger for another hour talking among themselves. There was great excitement about the opportunity to connect with likeminded people.

The second council meeting covered the early childhood education industry and was led by Roger Brown of Bright Horizons, Clark Adams of Mulberry Schools, and Rosemary Jordano of Children First. The quarterly meetings to follow covered such topics as the test prep market and charter schools run by for-profit companies.

By 2000, GBEIC had over 100 members, and EduVentures benefited from this networking for business development in its own backyard. The individuals involved with the Greater Boston Education Industry Council exemplified the characteristics and personalities of some of the industry's true education entrepreneurs. The characteristics of the emerging education entrepreneurs were slightly different from a classic definition of an entrepreneur. The education market was uniquely more collegial and inclusive than most business sectors, and the entrepreneurs attracted to this space who would be most successful exhibited several key traits.

The most important driver was passion. This is the defining characteristic of a successful entrepreneur. First impressions of entrepreneurs are based largely on the passion they exhibit, followed by conviction, energy, and enthusiasm. Education poses its own set of challenges, so in addition to this fire in the belly, education entrepreneurs have to be singularly focused with a compelling vision. Education involves unique political challenges and lengthened decision-making time. Many of the early education entrepreneurs were driven by idealism, passionately desiring to improve education and opportunities for children—in other words, many shared the optimism that private ventures could generate public good.

Another memorable common trait of the education entrepreneurs who participated in the GBEIC was curiosity. Curiosity often results in creativity and innovation. It is an essential trait for future successful education entrepreneurs, unwilling to accept the status quo, and who advocate change while pursuing realistic and attainable goals. It is a balance of both idealism and pragmatism that makes successful education entrepreneurs. Education entrepreneurs should build diverse coalitions to achieve their goals because the market is not simply about the products or services, but must embody the value of helping kids, while generating revenues and profits.

But while idealism is admirable, the ultimate barometer of success in business, whether in education or elsewhere, is shareholder satisfaction. The most successful education entrepreneurs were those who found ways to align their passion for education with the discipline required by the competitive marketplace. This required welcoming the signals of profit versus loss and allowing this feedback to shape how ideals were pursued in practice. Idealism and camaraderie is nice, but ultimately success is measured in profits.

The GBEIC became a gathering point where many of the best education entrepreneurs assembled. Members demonstrated how successful education entrepreneurs could bring together passion, vision, curiosity, perseverance, and discipline to succeed in unique ways. Roger Brown and Linda Mason (Bright Horizons) focused on a big idea of providing childcare as a benefit provided by corporate employers. Houghton Mifflin's Nader Dareshori understood the limitations of the parochial ways of the publishing industry and went outside the box to form an incubator fund for investments in new education technology products and services. David Blohm had the curiosity and creativity to understand that his proprietary IQ test could be the foundation piece for an online store selling education testing and assessment products. Before funding Edison Corporation as a school management business, Chris Whittle established an innovative education business called Channel 1, which was ahead of its time in providing information to parents, teachers, and students via closed circuit television in schools. He saw K-12 as a market opportunity while others waited and wrung their hands. Jonathan Greyer of Kaplan Education presented his vision for building the business in both higher education and K-12 as a division of the Washington Post Company.

While some of these entrepreneurs succeeded more than others, they all possessed the persistence, focus, and fire in the belly to build a team and execute an idealistic, compelling vision.

SIZING THE EDUCATION MARKET

In 1997, *The Boston Business Journal* ran a major story on the for-profit education business percolating in Boston. EduVentures sent out several thousand copies of this article with a research report. This first research report was branded as a Research Brief and covered detailed market size and statistics. It was produced to differentiate EduVentures from *The Education Industry Report* newsletter. We wanted to position ourselves as a research-based consulting firm. EduVentures planned to focus on a singular report that would position itself and define the industry. So we seized this opportunity to publish the product that would replace The Education Industry Directory: a major annual overview of the market, its size by sector, and opportunities.

EduVentures' goal was to establish key facts and metrics and continue to repeat them, until everyone would state the information and note that it came from EduVentures. This would serve to build the brand. The more EduVentures was quoted, the more it would build credibility and, in a sense, "own" the data and numbers produced. This collection of data added to our competitive advantage. It wasn't that we were creating new information, but rather we served as a hub for all information to filter through. I often looked at research companies in the healthcare industry as a model.

EduVentures issued press releases verifying the research and numbers validated by other third parties, which enhanced the image and reputation of EduVentures. Third party verification helped build a brand that would be valued for the credibility of its product. The investment drivers and market trends provided the authoritative edge that the investment community needed for investment criteria. EduVentures was the first company to identify and size the sectors of the burgeoning market; our information steered many of the investors first entering the industry.

Below is how EduVentures reported data on the education market for 1996. It was our first effort at research that sized the market and its opportunities. The report gave the reader a quick elevator ride with crisp copy and impressive statistics that helped create the buzz for the industry.

The information contained in this report and future Eduventures products was frequently used as references in IPO registration documents, Wall Street investment bank books, private placement memorandums, entrepreneurs' business plans, books, and education policy papers. They became the gold standard for market sizing and clearly attracted business to the company.

EDUVENTURES 1996 RESEARCH BRIEF OVERVIEW

The United States spends $650 billion per year on education. Education spending is growing at a rate of 3–4 percent annually. In contrast, the "education industry"—which we define as representing the total revenues of for-profit education companies—is growing over 25 percent per year and surpassed $52 billion in 1996.

There are other important differences between the $650 billion of total education spending and the education industry besides rate of growth. While overall spending is concentrated on K-12, it accounts for only 1.2 percent of industry revenues. The largest concentration of for-profit companies is in areas not traditionally served by government, such as products, child care, enrichment services, corporate training, and post-secondary vocational education.

The education industry can be broken down into three main sectors: schools, services, and products. This research brief provides a breakdown of key take-aways and sectors. Education is already big business: With $650 billion in total expenditures, education is an established and large sector of the economy, commanding 9.7 percent of GDP (second only to healthcare).

At that time, the increasing importance of education to career success was becoming extremely apparent. No longer could a high school student count on a lifelong, dependable income with solely a high school diploma. As society and work began to center more around information, knowledge becomes even more key to professional success. But at the same time, the dual pressures of rising costs and the poor results of public education were creating opportunities for the private sector. The growing percentage of women in the work force increases demand for child care, immigration patterns grew the need for language instruction. and increasing numbers of adjudicated youth created higher demand for at-risk youth services.

THE SCHOOL SECTOR

The school sector consists of companies that own and/or operate child-care centers, K-12 proprietary or public schools, and post-secondary proprietary schools.

Child care companies. These companies, with total revenues of $12 billion, serve children ages 0 to 5 in stand-alone sites, office park centers, and/or employer-sponsored centers. Its growth drivers were the increasing participation of women in the workforce, more companies extending benefit offerings to include child care, and increasing recognition of the importance of early childhood education.

K-12 Proprietary and Privately-Managed Public Schools. These companies include proprietary schools and charter and traditional public schools that are operated by private companies, such as The Edison Project and Education Alternatives. Total revenues in this segment were $637 million, or less than .2 percent of total K-12 education expenditures in the early 1990s. Its growth drivers were parent dissatisfaction with traditional public education, growing interest in experiments with charter schools, and possibly (though not conclusively) vouchers.

Post-secondary Schools. These schools offer academic and vocational degree programs to high school graduates. Total revenues in 1996 were $3.5 billion. Its growth drivers were the increasing importance of technical skills for entry-level jobs, cuts in state funding of community colleges, a 20 percent rise in the number of high school graduates, and the high cost of non-profit private universities and colleges.

Educational Products Sector. The products sector had revenues of $21.2 billion in 1996 and included the largest and most established education companies in the industry. These companies faced no significant competition from the public or non-profit sectors, but rather service them by providing electronic media, traditionally published materials, and classroom supplies.

U.S. Expenditures in the school sector totaled $21.7 Billion in 1996.

THE PRODUCTS SECTOR

The educational products sector had revenues of $21.2 billion in 1996 and included the largest and most established education companies in the industry. These companies faced no significant competition from the public or non-profit sectors, but rather serviced them by providing electronic media, traditionally published materials, and classroom supplies.

Electronic Media. These companies, with 1996 sales of $2.2 billion, provided software, CD-ROM, video, laser disc, and Internet-delivered products to the school and home markets. Its growth drivers were developments in hardware support new media, larger installed base in homes creates demand for consumer education software, parents demand school technology, and more states include technology in statewide curriculum adoptions, and Internet buzz.

Traditional Publishing. Publishing companies focused on the sale of textbooks and other curriculum-based print materials, though they also published multimedia content. Publishers' sales in 1996 were $8.5 billion. Its growth drivers were mainly from the increase in the number of school-age children and from increased demand for printed instructional materials in the areas of adult education, vocational training, and home study.

Diversified Products. These products included hardware to the school market (computers, VCRs, and televisions), hand-held learning aids, flash cards, manipulative, and school supplies. Revenues in 1996 were $11 billion.

Educational Services. The services sector had revenues of $15.3 billion in 1996. Companies in this sector provided educational services paid for directly by the consumer or through a contract with a public entity. The three main services provided are training, management of at-risk services, and other diversified services.

Total U.S. expenditures in the products sector totaled $69.2 billion in 1996.

THE SERVICES SECTOR

Training. These companies, with 1996 sales of $12.8 billion, provided instructor-led, video-based, Internet-delivered, and/or computer-based training to professionals. Programs are not degree-granting, but often do offer licensure and certification. While overall U.S. training expenditures are over $58.9 billion, the industry share is 22 percent. Its growth drivers were fast-changing technology that requires employees to update skills, increasing demand for technical skills, corporate downsizing and outsourcing, and shortfalls of secondary education in preparing students for the workplace.

At-risk youth services. At-risk companies provide educational and rehabilitative services to at-risk and/or adjudicated youth. They may own their own facilities, contract with school districts, or contract with the juvenile justice system. Revenues for 1996 were $472 million, less than 6 percent share of the total U.S. expenditures of $8 billion. Its growth drivers were the dramatic increase in youth crime, high cost of government-run special education, baby boom echo, and an increasing propensity for governments to contract services.

Diversified Services: With $2.3 billion in sales, these companies offer enrichment courses, language instruction, remediation, after-school and summer programs, tutoring and test preparation, and contracted services with school districts, such as Title 1 and ESL instruction. Its growth drivers were tutorials and test preparation supplement shortfalls of public education, immigration causing need for ESL instruction, baby boom echo increasing college admissions competition, and a growing willingness of schools to contract out instruction.

GENERATING INVESTOR INTEREST

If one of the purposes of these reports was to create investor interest, than it succeeded. It is interesting to observe that the overall K-12, post-secondary, and publishing sectors have approximately doubled in the past twelve years to over $100 billion, which reflects stable growth of approximately 3–4 percent. This growth and total figure of $100 billion does not include the childcare market at $22 billion, which is now tracked and sized as a separate sector within education. Also, training is now regarded as a separate market and no longer considered part of the education market.

As a result of the charter school movement, K-12 schools revenues have growth from less than $1 billion to $15 billion. Approximately 10 percent of the 4,500 charter schools are operated by for-profit companies. For-profit post secondary schools are now a $19 billion market and there is a $2 billion market of online universities. This comparable number in 1996 was $3.5 billion in revenues.

The product sector has remained stable, growing at a 3–4 percent rate with greater use of Internet-based technology products and consistent school adoption of textbooks. The largest growth sector other than schools is the service sector with the alternative school and for-profit special education market reaching $5 billion in 2008. In addition, the tutoring market to both consumers and schools was a $3 billion market in 2008.

A DOT-COM STORY

By the 1990s, tutoring businesses were flourishing in countries such as India, South Korea, and Israel; it was clear there would soon be significant growth in the States. In 1997, David Blohm, owner of Virtual Knowledge, approached EduVentures to help establish a business plan and strategy to bring the company to scale, as well as to assist the company in fundraising. David had purchased control of Virtual Knowledge from its two founders who had developed proprietary software and a CD-ROM for self-paced testing, including a variety of products for career advancement, tutoring, and test preparation.

One of the company's products was able to test a child's aptitude to the point of being recognized as a norm-based test for IQ. As a technology software expert, David had the vision that this series of test products could be produced and marketed to parents to work with their children for college preparation. David was able to convince Sylvan Learning Systems and a few of his technology software friends and family friends to invest in Virtual Knowledge.

David is a prime example of an entrepreneur with a proven track record who could present his company vision and plan clearly. He was innovative and persistent and singularly focused on the outcome of taking the company public. Working with David was an extraordinarily interesting experience and promised to be profitable, because not only did EduVentures earn significant consulting and advisory fees, but we also retained equity shares and options in Virtual Knowledge in lieu of cash payments. In 1997 the name of the company was changed from Virtual Knowledge to SmarterKids.com. A Web site was created and the company developed a series of products and plans to become the superstore of education improvement products. Through their internal research they had created their version of a "Good Housekeeping" seal of approval for each one of their products.

The company had a great motto: "When it comes to kids and education, one size does not fit all." As part of their Web site, they created a personalized store for every child. This type of marketing was way ahead of its time. The self-paced IQ test was their biggest seller and laid the foundation for education testing, assessment, and self-improvement products for both the parent and the consumer. In 1997, company revenues were approximately $1.4 million, and in May 1999, they went public. This was the dot-com era, and every parent wanted smarter kids. Wall Street loved it!

The initial public offering of SmarterKids.com was quite a lesson in Wall Street corporate finance. EduVentures' shares and options received were valued at more than $1 million at the time of the IPO. Unfortunately, Wall Street's positive response was based more on hope and expectation than on understanding of the emerging education market. Everyone had a lot to learn. As original shareholders, EduVentures was obligated to a six-month lock-up, making us unable to sell our shares until after six months and one day from the time of the initial offering. By that time, the shares had lost 95 percent of their value. This was the dot-com era—it was not unusual for an Internet company to skyrocket and crash all within a six-month period. The understanding of a lock-up period for original investors in an IPO is an important lesson.

Despite the ultimate financial disappointment of the SmarterKids.com offering, 1997 was a banner year for EduVentures. The company was engaged by several firms to identify potential acquisitions and partnerships, matching the company's investing priorities with prospects that best fit these priorities and the purchasing company's environment. Among deals in the late 1990s was identifying and closing an acquisition by Mulberry Childcare Centers for a chain of childcare outlets in Arizona and providing consulting and research for Corporate Family Solutions, which ultimately merged with Bright Horizons. EduVentures also represented a Toronto company, International Business Schools on the sale of their for-profit, post-secondary business to a private investment firm. Other early year involvements included Carole Valone, who founded the technology platform company Web CT, which ultimately merged with Blackboard to become the leading delivery system for course management systems for college and universities around the world.

TURNING POINT

The year 1997 also was a turning point for EduVentures. It was clear the company's efforts and publicity were gaining a competitive advantage of being the go-to middleman. The advisory business was growing. EduVentures worked to be recognized as the company who is the friend of the entrepreneur—the education entrepreneur.

At the time, interested parties from the United States and around the world were beating a path to the EduVentures door, initially because of the January 1996 *New York Times* article, and later because of the publicity of our 1996 market research brief. Unsolicited calls were constant—the vetting process became a challenge. Qualifying a lead in a collegial field like education can be frustrating. In many ways, educators and even entrepreneurs view each other as colleagues, not competitors, making it difficulty to get unvarnished, accurate information.

The expense and time of sifting out calls and separating ideas and concepts from real businesses was significant. At that time there was no protocol for communicating with outside interested parties as there is today. Today it is simple: a prospective client can send an e-mail with an attached PDF of their business plan or an executive summary. When EduVentures began, though, client acquisition was grassroots, and most initial communication was done face-to-face or by phone and required a quick analysis to determine whether it was worth pursuing. It was not an efficient process, and there was a lot of time spent with "tire kickers" seeking free advice. Being a part of the Greater Boston Education Industry Council (GBEIC) provided us focus and greater freedom to pick and choose our projects. EduVentures had decided against being a bank or a private equity fund—we would maximize shareholder value in other ways.

By late 1997, EduVentures had established enough of a reputation and built a staff to be in the unique position of being able to focus on clients with a high potential for success. Because of prohibitive cost and regulatory compliance, EduVentures had decided against becoming a broker dealer, so the company was not positioning itself as an investment bank. Rather, EduVentures served as a consultant and financial advisor to introduce companies to potential sources of capital and received our fees on a consultant basis rather than success fees.

In the beginning, being in the middle as an advisor, consultant, and champion of the industry would not provide large immediate returns, but with momentum building, it did provide the opportunity for long-term gains. EduVentures would never create an enterprise with the revenue potential of some of the larger companies and posed a challenge in trying to raise outside capital. The prospects of building a high growth, high-value enterprise were certainly attractive, but in the end, EduVentures' "niche" was in providing research, consulting, and advisory services.

The key factor in that decision was not to reposition our strategy as the industry "hub" of information by hiring and training new people with investment background experience. There was a concern that hiring and training

these people would potentially bring in people solely interested in wealth creation and not the company's mission. Interestingly this philosophy attracted a
unique breed of employees for EduVentures. The culture was purposeful, and
the employees' expectation of financial success was there, but it was coupled
with a sincere passion for the education industry and the company's position
as its independent, trusted source of information.

EduVentures continued to sharpen its focus to mining data that was
newsworthy and available at everyone's fingertips. The company worked to
build the largest proprietary database of industry companies and people. What
is the market? How big? Who are the players? Where are the opportunities?

EduVentures provided some due diligence research and advisory work for
investment banks and venture capital firms, but they were among the least profitable calls we received. An essential flaw in the investment banking system
is the orientation to a transaction that allocated little or no money for research
by an independent source. The investment firms did their own "sell-side"
research and therefore formed a bias for the stocks they covered. While this
posed an obvious conflict of interest, there was never a significant opportunity
for selling investment research in the for-profit education market.

Venture capital and private equity groups, seeking profitable acquisitions
in the market, appreciated the value of EduVentures' research, but frequently
did not have the cash on hand to spend for it. Their preference was to pay
for the work from the proceeds of a transaction. It is almost counterintuitive,
since ideally it would make sense to pay for information in advance to make
a better investment decision.

About this time, an investment firm in New York, Fulcrum Information
Services, began to schedule a series of national investment seminars called
the Education Industry Finance and Investment Institute. This first event
featured Sam Yau, CEO of National Education Services; Benno Schmidt,
who had recently resigned as the president of Yale to become the CEO
of the Edison Project; Eugene Hickok, secretary of state of education in
Pennsylvania; and Brett Schindler, the mayor of Jersey City, New Jersey.
EduVentures served as a co-sponsor of the event. It was the first of many
national events where industry leaders were able to meet with leaders of the
investment community.

DECISION TIME

Buzz about the growing education industry began to flow to Wall Street.
EduVentures seriously considered the possibility of an education industry
fund and engaged an experienced business development officer, David

Cappelluci as a consultant to pursue this idea. The ability to communicate with both entrepreneurs and investors continued to show us that EduVentures' best income opportunity was as an intermediary, rather than the principal, in an investment fund.

By early 1998, EduVentures' annual research brief on the industry focused on the industry and had begun to position the company as a major participant in the growth of the industry. In March 1998, the company sponsored a well-attended symposium on business and education that took place at Harvard's Kennedy School to honor David Kearns' historic career, tireless efforts, and accomplishments related to his roles in business, government, and education.

Two panel discussions focused on business and educational partnerships and the role of for-profit companies in education. Lamar Alexander offered the opening address, and the event mirrored the excitement and enthusiasm pulsing through the growing education industry at the time. Much of the discussion at this event also provided a better understanding of the realistic and attainable objectives and outcomes possible for America's business leaders in the education marketplace, whether the motives were financial, self interest, corporate public relations, or the new concept of social entrepreneurship. The conference would also provide an important serendipitous moment because of the attendance of Thomas Dretler, who was a family friend and who would come to play an important role in EduVentures.

After meeting Tom, it was evident how his interests and priorities aligned with EduVentures. Philosophically, we both believed that an enterprise could be based on the premise of a private venture for the public good while also generating profitable returns. I suggested a good exercise for us would be for Tom to write a memo on how he could help EduVentures "mine the gold."

The "mine the gold" memo ended up being be a running conversation as the plan developed to bring the company to scale and profitability. Tom joined EduVentures as the chief operating officer in July 1998. By this time, EduVentures had focused on financial advisory and consulting activities, but our vision was still ambitious, so we began to consider expanding and building offices outside of Boston. The most obvious choice for expansion seemed to be San Francisco.

Like Boston, San Francisco, had the somewhat unusual blend of a rich academic community, numerous venture capitalists, and a passionate and healthy-sized group of education entrepreneurs seeking capital and opportunities to build careers in the education industry. It seemed fertile ground for replicating the Greater Boston Education Industry Council, but we first needed to identify the size of the market opportunity in San Francisco. Two energetic entrepreneurs emerged in the Bay Area wanting to help organize the San Francisco Education Industry Council (SFEIC), James Sparkman and Scott Clegg. James was a Harvard Business School graduate, and Scott was the son of Jack Clegg, the CEO of Nobel Learning Company, a successful, publicly held K-12 proprietary school and childcare care company. James and Scott were anxious to help organize EduVentures West. At that point, the company secured the needed financial resources and put a management team in place, along with a plan to launch an EduVentures office in San Francisco.

EduVentures hired James Sparkman and leased a temporary office head-quarters there. As part of the kick-off, James began to organize a SFEIC. He worked from a list of clients and prospects, as well as members of the Association of Educators in Private Practice (AEPP). It seemed the prospective membership would provide a strong pipeline for EduVentures to put a local client "deal flow" in place.

Unfortunately, the decision for geographic expansion proved premature. While the West Coast was a dynamic marketplace, we were unable to satisfy James' entrepreneurial needs as he felt pulled to be in business for himself rather than open an EduVentures office. It was an important reminder that in a start-up venture, key employees' visions must be in sync with those of the founders. Without a serious team leader on the West Coast, EduVentures refocused its efforts and energies in the Boston area, though we eventually reconnected with James at a later date when he became an EduVentures client. The San Francisco efforts proved that early stage companies should be sensitive to making certain that key employees' expectations are aligned with management's. This is an important lesson for entrepreneurs as all expectations must be aligned at the beginning, with a clear understanding and agreement on issues such as title, role, and financial compensation.

With San Francisco behind us, it was time to get down to serious business of figuring out how to "mine the gold."

Chapter 6

Mining the Gold

Chapter 6 shows the importance of social entrepreneurs' need to balance their enthusiasm and vision with the trial and error process of developing sustainable and scalable models creating ultimate financial success. It offers a first-hand understanding of building a business, while navigating the "bust" period and the aftermath of 9/11. The chapter highlights the need for entrepreneurs to remain flexible and why this is particularly true in education where innovation and business discipline must be balanced. The Chapter also provides an early understanding of the Internet and its potential for delivery of information to a broad and diverse audience.

The term "mining the gold" became a popular saying at EduVentures in 1998. After Tom Dretler joined the team in July 1998, the management team was built in pursuit of this goal. The first hire was Peter Stokes, who had previously done consulting work with Tom. A former writing and literature teacher at Tufts University, Massachusetts College of Art, and the State University of New York at Stony Brook, Peter had worked to create online teaching courses at Lesley College and Stonehill College in the early 1990s. He also spent time as a manager of the industry research group at Daratech, Inc., making him the perfect fit for directing the company's research efforts and maintain our proprietary Education Industry Database.

Like any other small company, EduVentures tried to support its strategic model while maintaining monthly revenue to "keep the lights burning." The challenge was to create a delicate balance between maintaining revenues, while establishing a team to implement a sustainable model. Fortunately, because the EduVentures brand had been established, we were able to pursue consulting projects that had the potential both to keep the lights on and to provide us with working capital.

Many projects would follow over the transom because of the larger-than-life image that the media created for EduVentures. One such opportunity came from a company not even in the education field itself, but in health care and based in California. Tenet Health Care was a major manager and administrator of for-profit hospitals and healthcare facilities. Tenet knew of EduVentures' expertise in education and wanted to engage the company to explore how they could develop a plan and strategy to enter the education market. These types of projects were important since many companies were branching out and considering expanding to new markets, especially in an era where the Internet was becoming a crucial tool. The Tenet Project came as a result of press coverage and an article in *Fortune* magazine and was the first example of a business from outside the education industry approaching us to help them enter the market. Never underestimate the power of public relations.

In October 1998, under the direction of Peter Stokes, EduVentures launched *E-News & Views,* an e-mail publication created to test the potential as an Internet information provider. The late 1990s were a time of near endless optimism for opportunities arising from the Internet, and there seemed to be potential in this new channel of communication. The electronic newsletter was a free, bimonthly publication that was delivered to education industry stakeholders to provide a user-friendly management tool. The publication provided the industry with timely news summaries, original editorial content, and Web links to other education-related resources. The struggle was whether to offer a free or paid subscription newsletter. The concept of creating "eyeballs" and "impressions" won over the argument that clients should pay for the content. It was a battle that continues to be waged in new media. The free model was the correct decision if the Internet was going to become EduVentures' primary platform.

By late 1998, the first foray into the Internet showed impact. *E-News* attracted educational companies, policy researchers, government agencies, investors, and non-profit leaders on a global scale. But EduVentures' main objective was still to build a foundation for long-term clients. As a result, an opt-in subscription model was utilized, which meant that all subscribers had to enroll on a proprietary database. Within the first year the subscriber base was approximately 10,000 readers in thirty-eight countries.

At the time, the success of the newsletter provided the momentum needed to build an Internet information business, rather than seeking additional consulting clients. This fueled the March 1999 launch of EduVentures' *Online Investor,* a monthly publication read by several thousand education-industry investors, education entrepreneurs, and their companies. This newsletter was designed to facilitate financial transactions in the industry. In the spring of the same year, EduVentures also published *Management Source,* a Web-based communications channel and career development tool dedicated exclusively to the management needs of the education industry. Through the development of the *Management Source,* EduVentures had created a series of beta products designed to help the company develop a more comprehensive understanding of the online information business.

It was clear that EduVentures was changing to try to respond to the shifting landscape of the education industry. The Internet and technological revolution was also affecting everything. In order to succeed as a viable research company, the scope of the company's business needed to change. Tom Dretler believed the company should focus exclusively on the Internet. The issue became one of how to create a research-business model with a consistent and growing client base. The Internet would serve as the delivery mechanism to help "mine the gold" in the form of an Internet-based education portal. EduVentures business, like education itself, would continually be affected by the changing discourse on education reform and by the revolution in communications technology. As a result, the company's vocabulary, like its name, had to change. The name change from EduVentures to EduVentures.com was an easy transition to reflect a new focus primarily on the Internet. It seemed that the distinctions between public and private, or for-profit and not-for-profit, would continue to lose their force and meaning. The "education industry" was becoming a global education economy—an education economy which consisted of a complex network of institutions and businesses working to meet the challenges of education reform and improvement on a global scale.

EduVentures.com would need to be rebuilt to maximize growth potential. The allure of the dot-com boom captured us all. Using the Internet, a company could scale up faster and reach global markets. It provided the potential to take EduVentures.com from a smaller company to a multi-million dollar company in a shortened time frame. But to achieve this, new and significant investments were necessary. In the summer of 1999, a first private placement memorandum was written, and the company began to accrue initial investments for its new direction.

Part of the business plan was to develop a more comprehensive platform for the delivery of news and information. It became clear that education stakeholders suffered from fragmented research, high-costs, and a critical shortage of skilled management employees. What stakeholders needed most was a single point of entry into the education marketplace, where all their information needs could be met in one easy-to-use, easy-to-navigate, secure, online environment. The goal was to do this through a more complex Web site, but that couldn't be achieved without outside help. The development of a Web site and designing an online information delivery system was still a relatively new way to deliver information. Peter and Tom wanted Circle.com as their Web-design firm. Circle was the major media group firm owned by Arnold Advertising.

EduVentures.com was fortunate, through other business relationships, to line up a meeting with Ed Eskandarian, who was the chairman and CEO of Arnold & Co. and its subsidiaries, which included Circle.com. During our meeting with Ed and his Web-design team, Ed asked several questions to gain a better understanding of the market EduVentures.com was serving. In the course of a thirty-minute meeting, he deciphered what the participants in the education market needed most: access to high-quality information and data that was unbiased and informative. He also understood that the market was still emerging and potential customers needed to find ways to access capital as well as assistance in refining their own business models. In order to build a viable education company, clients would need to find talent and understand the skill-sets required for future education entrepreneurs.

This brief session with Ed was the value-added endorsement needed for EduVentures.com to make the decision to hire Circle as the Web-design firm. Conversations with Circle honed in on three key ideas: knowledge, capital, and management. By leveraging its proprietary research, rich database, and communication channels, EduVentures.com was able to provide the new education community with high quality online resources in its newly identified key issues: knowledge, which included market research, news, and information; capital, which included significant deal-flow opportunities and investment research; and management, with executive-and management-level tools.

EduVentures.com intended to fundamentally change the way education stakeholders communicated and did business. By building a Web-based resource with significant content and services, as well as access to the best-of-breed service providers in areas such as consulting, investment banking, and executive search, the company aimed to provide entrepreneurs, investors, and educators with the knowledge, capital, and management tools critical to their growth and success.

RAISING CAPITAL

Another important milestone leading up to our private placement memorandum dealt with EduVentures.com's shifting management. Tom and I discussed his move up to become the CEO of EduVentures.com. As part of this new arrangement, we would have to agree on my role relative to raising funds for the company. We agreed that I would assist him and the company by raising capital from my friends and business colleagues through a private placement memorandum. The caveat was that this would be a one-time request and that future company funding would be raised from institutional investors strictly based on the performance of the company.

Tom became the CEO, and as chairman of the board of the company, I took on the key role of raising working capital. The money began to flow; we hired additional staff, and we continued to reorganize the business to launch an Internet portal to the education industry. Revenues came from subscriptions to EduVentures.com's proprietary, syndicated content; from sponsorship agreements with education businesses; from other firms seeking to promote their offerings to the EduVentures.com community; and from conference registrants and exhibitors. The goal was to leverage proprietary research, grow the database of clients and prospects, get additional sponsorship, and continue the cycle by lowering subscription prices.

EduVentures.com also spun off a sister organization named EV Partners to serve as an entity to hold the education industry investments I had received since 1994 as part of consulting compensation. These initial assets of EV Partners were my own, including options to purchase shares from start-up ventures such as SmarterKids.com Inc., International Business Schools Inc., and Turnstone Publishing Group. Whenever I did business with small companies and entrepreneurs, I would attempt to make deals that included equity options for EV Partners. As an incentive for an investor's purchase into EduVentures.com, shareholders received a bonus in equity stakes in a small portfolio of early stage education companies through the ownership of EV Partners.

Following this first private placement memorandum, the excitement was growing. By the fall, several critical milestones were achieved, while remaining on budget:

- The monthly Web site hits increased by twenty-eight times to over 200,000.
- The monthly page views increased more than fifteen times to approximately 7,300.
- The readership of the leading education industry newsletter, *The Education Economy* was reaching an audience of over 10,000.
- The new Web site was launched three months before anticipated.
- The company upgraded its technology infrastructure to support accelerated growth.

Confidence was high that EduVentures.com would indeed become the major online information and research portal for the education industry. Our hope was to capitalize on our growing first-mover advantage, but we still needed to raise additional capital. In retrospect, it was fortunate that we did not raise more because cash fueled the temptation to spend, which was the norm of that era. It would have been relatively easy to spend $20 million rather than the $4 million raised.

RENEWING VISION, RENEWABLE REVENUE

Even with these successes, it soon became clear that being strictly an online research firm would not bring in enough revenue to be sustainable. In November of that year, EduVentures.com was redefined once again towards building a base of research subscribers who would create a source of dependable, renewable revenue. The driver again was to increase shareholder value. EduVentures.com would be a combination of a destination for quality research (a "Forrester Research" for the education industry) and an online portal—a gateway to voluminous information resources on the Web. EduVentures.com would have three distinct customer groups covering the realm of entrepreneurs (start-ups), investors (equity and banking), and educators (traditional institutions).

"Entrepreneurs" was an umbrella term EduVentures.com used to describe the universe of companies (both education companies and non-education companies) that we wanted to attract to our site for information on the education industry. This category included everything from start-up education companies who were writing business plans and attempting to raise capital, to world-renowned non-education companies such as Microsoft, Oracle, and Intel, all of whom viewed education as a key marketplace for their products and services.

"Investors" was the umbrella term used to describe the universe of venture capital and private equity firms, investment banks, and "angel" investors who were either specifically interested in sourcing education industry deals or had heard about the industry and wanted to get more information.

"Educators" described traditional educational institutions such as colleges and universities, public and private schools, non-profit organizations, think tanks, and government agencies affected by the education industry who benefited from access to information about it. This category represented a tremendous opportunity to expand and diversify our community of users, and we continually discussed opportunities to "open the tent" by inviting educators to join entrepreneurs and investors in the discussion on how the private sector could most effectively impact the education market.

Past experience suggested that education businesses interested in creating new opportunities were paying a significant price for market inefficiencies.

EduVentures.com addressed the market inefficiencies by providing entre-preneurs, investors, and educators with high-quality tools. EduVentures.com established itself not only as the world's most knowledgeable group on edu-cation industry markets and opportunities, but also as the premier aggregator of information in the industry. It was back to our strongest suit as the "hub" of the industry.

This comprehensive approach to the industry would serve the company well in the long run. Because of market fragmentation, there were many other players in the space, but none of them had been firmly established as a source of comprehensive information for the entire industry. They remained niche players, providing certain types of information, useful only to a portion of the audience EduVentures.com intended to serve.

As such, most of them could be considered "competitors" only in the sense that they published information relevant and valuable to the education indus-try. Nelson B. Heller & Associates, for example, published two print newslet-ters, *Educational Technology Markets* and *Internet Strategies for Education Markets,* and two e-mail-based products, *Desktop EdNET* and *EdNet Week Headlines.* Heller also sponsored the annual EdNet: Educational Technol-ogy and Telecommunications Markets Conference, and the EdNet Industry Awards Program, as well as provided consulting services to the education publishing, computer, financial services, software, and telecommunication industries.

Another competitor, *The Education Industry Report,* now John McLaugh-lin's company, was also a sole proprietorship based in Sioux Falls, South Dakota. The newsletter continued to feature industry transactions as well as an Education Industry Index, which tracked market performance of educa-tion companies. Similarly, Quality Education Data (QED), headquartered in Denver, Colorado, was a research and database company, focused exclu-sively on education. QED's National Education Database covered all U.S. and Canadian educational institutions and supported QED-market research, marketing databases, database design, and annual research reports tracking educational trends.

BUILDING CONTENT

Clearly, there was growing interest in participating in the education industry from a number of players and even sectors not traditionally associated with education. As the calendar rolled toward the year 2000, EduVentures.com continued to grow. In February 2000, it ventured back into familiar territory. In order to build a contact library and industry credibility, EduVentures.com formally announced the total acquisition of The Education Industry Group (EIG). John McLaughlin, who was the president at the time, would also join EduVentures.com's company's board of advisors. *The Education Industry Report* was once again an EduVentures.com-sponsored publication. The acquisition's objective was to acquire the archives and other content of the *Education Industry Report,* which would be used as support for subscription and research clients. McLaughlin's role was to train and advise research analysts. To some degree, the acquisition also was a strategic defensive move as the company was for sale, and EduVentures.com did not want that content to be in the hands of a potential competitor.

As part of building our content library, we also were interested in content and research in the education technology market. Consequently, it was at this time that EduVentures.com made plans to acquire one of its main competitors, Nelson B. Heller & Associates (NBH&A). Of particular interest was NBH&A's Heller Reports™, which were widely regarded as a major source of research in the industry. Acquiring The Heller Reports™ would have further expanded EduVentures.com offerings, while their EdNET division could have broadened the company's conference strategy. The deal seemed like a good fit, even though it never went through. Nelson Heller, as the founder and entrepreneur, was uncomfortable joining a firm with another education entrepreneur. As he correctly understood, the force and will of two competing entrepreneurs could lead to tension, and he was seeking to join his efforts to a more mature company that already had its vision, policy, and procedures in place.

A few years later, NBH&A was sold to Scholastic, which was a good fit for the owner and founder. Scholastic wanted to roll NBH&A into their Quality Education Division (QED). Heller was able to continue working in his style, while being part of a large corporate environment and reporting to a single manager.

In the early industry, most of the successful mergers actually involved an entrepreneur selling to a corporate partner rather than between entrepreneurs. This fostered easier transitions and merging of company cultures. In this scenario, owners would tell the partner how their business was to be run versus a clash of egos between entrepreneurs who viewed themselves as peers. Clashes between entrepreneurs (and their egos) is classic. It is always a potential reaction when the complex chemistries of two passionate and driven entrepreneurs meet.

For much of 2000 everything seemed to be going in the right direction. Although the dot-com bust had been in full swing for several months, EduVentures.com seemed to be shielded from it. The company had capital, direction, and was growing at a phenomenal rate. As a result, EduVentures.com was invited to present to the Ford Foundation. The Ford Foundation, one of the nation's largest and most highly regarded foundations, had reached out to us to help them understand exactly what the phenomenon called the education industry was. It was a significant compliment that a foundation of this importance would look to EduVentures.com as an authority on the for-profit education market.

The presentation illustrated how the education industry had arrived as a true sector of the United States economy, having consistently grown from the 1990s through to the early 2000s. The major market segments identified were: schools, products, services, and e-services. By 2004, the industry's market capitalization of $100 billion exceeded the industry's company revenues of $90 billion. This would mark an important milestone for the industry, as it began to signal to Wall Street a real opportunity for public investment, meaning that education companies could attract significant new capital to improve education. The concept of industry revenues versus public market valuation is important as a company tries to create liquidity and unlock the revenues of the industry's private companies into the public marketplace.

At that time, there were approximately sixty publicly held education-industry businesses. The largest were the major publishers and the for-profit higher education businesses. The company produced a report at a later date which was placed on the U.S. Department of Education Web site, titled *What Is the Education Industry?* The report broke down the market size and sectors according to all of EduVentures.com's numbers and became the most downloaded report from the DOE that year. It was another celebrated milestone. In order to maintain visibility you have to continually have your name appear to the potential customer either by print or online.

In January 2000, *Business Week* published its first article recognizing the growth of for-profit companies in education. The article noted a huge spike in annual private investments for the industry. Money from venture funds, leveraged buyouts, individual investors, and private sources was pouring into for-profit education companies. EduVentures.com was directly quoted in the article, and many of the figures and projections were based on our research. The general belief was that increases in enrollment and the Internet were going to revolutionize the industry. It was the first time the larger investment community recognized that education companies were emerging as a significant and compelling industry.

If one were to see education as a candidate for a publicly traded industry sector fund, the general rule of thumb was that there should be a publicly held market value equivalent to approximately two times the revenue of the privately held companies. This was the benchmark for Fidelity Investments, a pioneer and industry leader in this sector. EduVentures.com had been tracking the revenues of the private companies whose combined revenues were approaching the $100 billon range. At that time it meant that publicly held revenues should be approximately $200 billion to warrant establishing a specific industry sector fund. To date there has not been a publicly traded education industry sector fund to test this rule of thumb.

In July 2000, Circle's hard work on the Web site finally materialized. From their efforts, EduVentures.com was able to formulate an online strategy. With tools that promoted high quality business and investment decision making, the education industry would finally have a portal that met its needs. Edu-Ventures.com now provided a wealth of information and services, including the following:

- *Strategic Research Reports.* Comprehensive strategic analysis and fore-casts of market trends, along with in-depth assessments of current market events and issues affecting industry insiders.
- *Industry Analyses.* Weekly electronic briefs that provided short, timely, expert perspectives on the competitive landscape and trends in the market-place.
- *Networking Opportunities.* Forums held at EduVentures.com-produced events that fostered business relationships among leading education profes-sionals and supported the dissemination of market knowledge to EduVen-tures.com subscribers.
- *Industry Events.* Access to the education and training industry's premier conferences and events worldwide.
- *Online Directories.* Access to thousands of industry contacts at key com-panies and investment firms.
- *Company Profiles.* Concise descriptions of the business and financial per-formance of leading education companies, as well as a critical assessment of each organization's competitive strengths and challenges.
- *Analyst Access.* Inquiry access to pose specific questions to senior analysts regarding research reports, strategic company profiles, or industry headlines.

The service was tiered, with less expensive subscriptions allowing limited access and more expensive subscriptions granted complete access. The price of the subscriptions varied between $1,000 and $10,000, depending on the report availability and the level of access to EduVentures.com consultants. The majority of subscribers would be at the lower price point, but it was hoped that gains in their confidence level would lead them to upgrade at a later date. Sure enough, such results materialized, and so the challenge became being able to develop additional content to support the higher tier subscription price. EduVentures.com landed several key clients during that time, including A&E Television, Bank of America, Blackboard, Inc., IBM, *New York Times,* The Princeton Review, and PriceWaterhouseCoopers.

At this point, EduVentures.com decided to professionalize our board of directors from a family board to a truly functional and independent board. The selection of new board members would be a key to the long-term success of the company. Transitioning from founder to CEO to chairman of the board and beyond is an important transition that requires careful and deliberate planning of governance and long-term strategy

The company was fortunate enough to attract two top-notch individuals to help during this period. Alan LeBovidge, who had recently retired as vice chairman of PricewaterhouseCoopers, agreed to come in as an independent director and assist in building the necessary systems for financial management and control within the company. Alan also became the mentor of the company's chief accounting officer, which was extremely important during the difficult years following the heady dot-com boom. Les Charm, a highly regarded professor of entrepreneurship at Babson College, accepted a position on the new board following Alan's departure and made enormous contributions to the company. Les brought practical experience as a seasoned academic and entrepreneur who understood the education market. Having Alan and Les's input was invaluable, as start-up companies can greatly benefit from the expertise and wisdom of experienced board members. Building a strong board of directors is an important first step for education entrepreneurs who are establishing their business.

One of the board's first tasks was to take a long hard look at EduVentures. com's business model in terms of the content that was being delivered, based on the original market need analysis of the three key issues: knowledge, capital, and management. Based on the response of paid subscribers, the most sought after information was for knowledge-based research and reports which were reaching a significant majority of the audience. It was the greatest profit contributor, and client feedback was highly favorable.

On the other hand, capital research published to help the investment community turned out to be a sticky legal challenge, particularly because the company was not registered as a broker dealer. The Securities and Exchange Commission (SEC) has strict rules on consulting firms selling investment information without proper authorization. EduVentures.com was able to sell subscriptions to venture capital and private equity firms, but it quickly realized that their needs were short-term oriented as they were seeking a one- time list of prospective investments. They were not really interested in comprehensive, detailed research. Soon after the boom period in the education industry ended, the capital research channel of the company's Web site was eliminated.

We had similar challenges with the management research channel as the industry was not yet mature enough to support the outside fees associated with adding more staff. The large publishing companies and many smaller, entrepreneurial start-up ventures already dominated the industry. EduVentures.com became primarily a networking force, and it seemed that the company was, unfortunately, too far ahead of the online social networking phenomenon. It was determined that the management-level career subscription tools would also be removed from the Web site as the company began to focus on its enhanced research subscription.

A TIPPING POINT FOR THE WORLD, AND AN INDUSTRY

On September 11, 2001, everything changed. That catastrophic event not only traumatized America and the world, but also became the tipping point for EduVentures.com and the education industry. The decline of employment and business activity in the boom of education market finally caught up with the larger slowing economy, and things slowed to a standstill.

At the time, the company used a free newsletter called *Education Economy* (with about 10,000 subscribers) to comment on major world issues and their impact on education and to assure the market and the community that in the end, education is always the best route to broaden knowledge and deepen understanding. In many ways this effort, though not a direct revenue driver, was an example of using private ventures to create public good.

For EduVentures.com, fiscal reality started to creep in. The company had ample cash reserves, but the dramatic downturn in business was not forecasted and the company needed to adjust budget and cash flow projections. Tom Dretler rose to the occasion with the assistance of the board. But there were no other sources of capital. The issue was not only finding a way to keep the lights on, but to also reassure employees and clients that we were financially sound. The company had to maintain momentum and provide continuity while sustaining the business during this challenging time.

The post-9/11 slow down brought the lessons from the dot-com bust to the forefront. The generational divide within the company (most of our employees were under thirty) became a driver for how we would work through the weeks ahead. The dot-com bust and new economic circumstances enabled those of us with many years in business to demonstrate that constructive things would come from those life experiences, as there is no substitute for experience.

Despite the turbulence, it seemed likely that EduVentures.com would become a successful business and that the company had more purpose than simply championing the size of our industry and its enormous potential. The burden of having outside shareholders superseded the prestige of being able to tell others that EduVentures.com was going to become a huge company. Having a small and profitable business was more important.

PATH TO PROFITABILITY

It was impossible to offer the lowest price on all education industry products, so the objective became very simple: to find a gross profit margin, stick to it, and control expenses so that our bottom-line operating margins would reach our objectives. It sounds very simple, but this was not an era of simplicity. This was the beginning of an experimental information era. Few businesses had determined how to translate the hits, visits, and page views of a Web site into revenue generation. In many companies, expenses ran rampant and operating for-profit became a luxury. The dot-com era was simply not singularly focused on operating profitable companies.

With a redefined focus exclusively on revenue generating, sales grew in 2001. A significant percentage of original clients were renewed, and new clients and new markets were identified. In 2002, the company continued to grow and, because of the subscription model, were able to be cash-flow positive while incurring a minor loss. As a subscription-based business, clients paid their subscription fee up front. Customers' cash was a helpful source to fund our operation.

One of the strategic moves in 2002 was to partner on a six-figure deal with Reed Exhibitions (a division of Reed Elsevier Corporation) to outsource the operation and financial risk of EduVentures.com's conferences. The company became the content partner and committed to expand some of the well-known conference titles, such as *The Digital Education Marketplace* and *The Future of Higher Education*. It was back to basics in terms of research and consulting, which freed up a tight cash position. In 2003, cash-flow growth increased and modest profits were generated. By 2004, the company not only generated more cash, but also enjoyed profit margins of close to 10 percent.

THE SALE OF EDUVENTURES

In the fall of 2003, I spent a six-month period in New York City, analyzing the potential for redevelopment of a scalable research product for the investment community. EduVentures.com's prospective clients included investment banks, private equity companies, angel investors, venture capital firms, and strategic investors. In the end, while there was a good amount of interest, there was still not a significant market willing to pay a fair price for the information alone. During those six months in New York, through my contacts in the investment community there, I made connections with people who expressed sincere interest in acquiring EduVentures.com. This was validation that the company's newest offerings to the higher education market had great potential and increased shareholder value.

It was during this time that Tom and the board decided that because we were not strictly an Internet company that we would drop the ".com" portion of our name and use Eduventures, Inc. It was clear that the K-12 market was a significant challenge for investors after the dot-com bust; a challenge that had been anticipated as a specific subscription offering to the higher education market was developed. The Eduventures' Higher Education Learning Collaborative ended up becoming the company's crown jewel. We left open the decision about what to do with our existing K-12 business for the longer term.

Knowledge Investment Partners (KIP) was an education-industry holding company with its own private investment fund. KIP's CEO, Bob Daugherty, felt that Eduventures, Inc. could be used as their platform for information and research on the education industry. KIP also had its own education-industry fund of publicly held companies. KIP had numerous investors in its fund, including the INVUS Group, an international private investment fund with several billion dollars of investments. One of Invus's holdings was Weight Watchers, Inc., which some financial analysts considered to be an education-industry company.

Eduventures had achieved dramatic growth (over 60 percent in 2004) and significant profits. Now was the time for a change of ownership and a whole new vision for the future of Eduventures.

In December 2005, the sale of Eduventures, Inc. to KIP who in turn, brought in the INVUS Group (as majority shareholders) was completed, allowing all original shareholders to exit from their original investment. This paved the way for Eduventures' board and management to again reassess the company's business strategy. The education industry was still emerging, and many of the key players were involved in direct competition with other leaders in their particular sector of the industry. The burden for was attempting to sell syndicated research to large groups of clients and particularly in the K-12 market sector. While the clients were most interested in our information and data, they were often unwilling to share confidential information with companies they considered to be competitors. This is particularly true in the K-12 market as it is larger and more fragmented. There was a strong fear in the industry that information would end up in the hands of their competitors. They wanted the benefit of Eduventures' historic research information and knowledge, but were greatly concerned that anything they shared would impact their competitive position. Would it be possible to get clients to become more collaborative and willing to share information?

And while the K-12 market was larger, it was more fragmented. Higher education was sufficiently mature to permit the sharing of research and information. Attention was focused on the higher education market due to the large and satisfied client base, particularly in the areas of continuing education and online learning.

The healthcare field offered insights, where research firms used a subscription model to get companies to collaborate. In this industry, the clients were willing to share information and used the research company as their trusted expert. Whatever was considered the clients' highest priority served as the basis for the activities of the research company. Like the healthcare industry, Eduventures began to think about how the company could leverage its brand to develop a similar model. Research that is directed and useful on a macro level is far more profitable than individualized publications.

Eduventures focused on two companies in the healthcare field, The Advisory Board and the Corporate Executive Board, to find a sustainable model that had scale and generated significant profit margins. The Advisory Board Company served a membership of leading hospitals, health systems, universities, and other mission-driven enterprises in the United States. Their goal was to use a collaborative model to provide an array of services, including research, executive education and leadership development, decision-support tools, and consulting. The Corporate Executive Board was a spin-off of The Advisory Board, which proved their model could work in other contexts, as they provided best-practices research, decision-support tools, and executive education to the greater corporate community.

These companies had significant financial success and were trading at very high, comparable shareholder valuations. To assess whether these models could translate. we had identified the similarities between the healthcare industry and education. Also at the time, EduVentures branding became an issue as the company moved farther into the higher education space. While the company had a highly recognizable brand, it was still recognized more in the K-12 field than in higher education. In the emerging K-12 market many clients were very competitive and unwilling to work collaboratively. Yet, in higher education the players felt more comfortable sharing information. They were willing to work with an outside authority and expert as their primary source of research and consultative support.

Eduventures' Higher Education Learning Collaborative program had found its niche. The intention was to continue the K-12 education-industry practice, but to also focus resources and efforts on higher education. Eduventures would become the expert in the middle, where clients would come together to share their best practices. The member-based research consortia would help to identify best management practices, track performance, and improve the organizational structure in higher education. Beyond programs in continuing education and online learning, the company developed numerous successful programs, each with between fifty and a hundred members from colleges and universities. The new programs were in the area of development, enrollment management, academic affairs, and schools of education. With the steady growth and potential in higher education, the Learning Collaborative was a success and ultimately became the core offering of Eduventures, Inc.

THE BALANCE OF PLANNING AND FLEXIBILITY

Figuring out how to mine the gold during Eduventures' first decade was a learning experience for all of us. There is no substitute for planning and teamwork. A company needs staying power that comes not only through access to capital, but also through the commitment of management for the long-term. The management and leaders need to have tough stomachs and the ability to react quickly. Tom Dretler and Peter Stokes have stayed the course for over a decade. A company must persist and persevere until the financial objectives are met. In a new venture, the two most important assets are a business model that is well thought through and a management team committed to the implementation of the model. Successful entrepreneurs cannot be distracted by short-term solutions.

While it is important to have a big idea, there is always a delicate balance to maintain between entrepreneurial creativity and the feasibility of implementing ideas. An idea that is too big can hamper the development of a clear business model. An idea too small can leave the entrepreneur and his team with too little interest to stay fully engaged in the learning process. A good business model needs to be scalable, and the business plan should show realistic and attainable goals and financial performance numbers. At Eduventures, as with any company with outside shareholders, it was important for management to feel pressured into attaining the results based on the projections in the private placement memorandum.

It is very important to be flexible, considering the dynamics of the marketplace. All of the early education companies faced particular challenges as the market they were serving was not fully defined. For Eduventures, these challenges were especially significant as the company had set out to build a business while defining an emerging and rapidly evolving industry. In addition to balancing creativity and practicality, we needed to balance staying focused while staying nimble. To the credit of the management team, this delicate balance was clear. At crunch time it was easy to turn on a "dime," which is something the company did many times following the dynamics of the nascent education industry.

In many ways Eduventures' trials and tribulations during the dot-com era mirrored those of the companies covered through our research. The major challenge was achieving profitability, while branding the company as the respected research authority in the market. The journey was not an easy one, but keeping balance during that time was a great life lesson for all those involved. By staying in business and not giving the slightest impression to the marketplace or our shareholders of the stressful journey, we knew that we had cleared an important hurdle. This was not the ultimate success, but it was an important milestone toward the original goal of having a highly successful enterprise that would promote the public good of improving education.

Chapter 7

Boom, Bust, and Unforeseen Consequences

Chapter 7 presents an overview of the impact of technology and the Internet on education and learning and provides a better understanding of the investment whims and criteria of the venture capitalist. The charter foreshadows the emergence of social entrepreneurs who funded foundations to support charter schools. It illustrates the power of the markets in determining what works and what does not work during the business cycles of a boom-and-bust period. It shows the reader the limitations of financial capital without human capital, the reality that entrepreneurs are often too far out front, and that the markets are the final arbiter. The chapter traces the industry's history from the beginning and how it evolved from textbook publishers and school-supply distribution, to entrepreneurs creatively developing products and services to benefit education and the emergence of the online education markets.

Even in the early 1990s, it wasn't yet possible to talk about the "education industry" or even "education entrepreneurship" in the way that is possible today. Through its high profile effort to raise a significant pool of funds for investment in educational innovation, the New American Schools initiative helped pave the way for innovative ways of thinking about raising financial and intellectual capital for education. When this unprecedented effort focused corporate philanthropy on the problems of our nation's schools, many education entrepreneurs and investors came to believe that bringing dramatic and replicable changes in education would require resources on a scale only Wall Street could provide. Of course, tapping these resources would require bringing to education the entrepreneurial and business tactics that worked to produce value in so many other American industry sectors.

As investors began to sniff around for profitable investment and business opportunities, there was optimism but uncertainty. Could private ventures undertaken for the public good, but disciplined by competition in a for-profit environment, achieve what public and corporate philanthropy had been unable to accomplish? Could the creative powers of entrepreneurs devise new approaches to education reform for the 21st century? These are the questions that surrounded the founding and evolution of Eduventures, Inc.

Eduventures recognized that private investment in for-profit education companies was going to be critical if education was going to successfully develop into a truly thriving and independent sector of the U.S. economy. Yet, there was very little private sector understanding of the business of education and scant empirical data on which to base investment decisions. Eduventures' work researching and tracking investment data for the education industry played an important role to both the industry itself and the investment community.

In order for education to make the transition from an emerging industry into a sustainable one, it would be necessary for many of these private investments to ultimately be converted into publicly-held companies. The vast resources that could convert small-scale innovation into system-wide transformation would be available primarily in public markets. Tens of thousands of private practitioners, in areas such as tutoring and special education, owned small businesses ,but the question was whether they could grow to a scalable level? It was unclear if these entrepreneurs, supported by new capital, could help create an industry.

According to the investment banks that covered education, the market value of stocks in an industry sector fund should be about two to three times the combined education businesses' revenues. Calculating a target market value in a sector where the majority of expenditures originated in government rather than business revenues is difficult. An unscientific method of calculating this measurement was to assume a need for $100 billion in revenues of education businesses and thus a corresponding target stock market valuation of $200–$300 billion. The $100 billion figure represented 10 percent of education expenditures of about $1 trillion.

In 1996, the market capitalization of education businesses totaled $60 billion, and before the public market's precipitous decline in 2001, Eduventures had forecast that total market capitalization would achieve the $200–$300 billion target (based on $100 million total revenue). This was quite possible given the existence of thousands of small, privately held education companies that might ripen for conversion through an IPO.

Today, that target of $200–$300 billion in stock market values for U.S. education companies remains far out of reach. As of the fall of 2008, the market cap of education industry companies covered by the investment firms Signal Hill and R.W. Baird, who write free monthly industry newsletters, is approximately $100 billion. Even if all of the largest, privately held companies such as Kaplan, Laureate, and Knowledge Universe were to become publicly held, the total market capitalization, including all the education publishers, would still be in the range of $150 billion. Where did the forecasting go so wrong? While technology and the Internet boom showed enormous promise, in the end education businesses demonstrated a lower rate of growth and did not achieve scale until a decade later.

THE RESEARCH

To look at the future, it would be instructive to look back at the past. Eduventures' research dated back to the early 1980s, beginning with the National Commission on Excellence in Education's 1983 report, *A Nation at Risk*. While this seminal report drew significant attention from the education and business communities, investors responded with only nominal investments into the education market, totaling less than $2 billion, and most of them fell into three sectors: schools, services, and products.

THE SCHOOL SECTOR

Most of the investments in education when *A Nation at Risk* was published in the 1980s were focused on existing brick and mortar businesses. Some of the notable early investments were in post-secondary vocational schools, such as those by Stonington Partners, an affiliate of Merrill Lynch. Stonington funded Education Management, which was later taken public and, in 2006, taken private again by Merrill Lynch with Goldman Sachs, Providence Equity Partners, and other investors in a transaction valued at $3.4 billion. Stonington also acquired Lincoln Tech, which operates schools for automotive, technology, and culinary arts. Lincoln Tech is now publicly held under the symbol of LINC.

This era also saw the emergence and growth of several vocational trade schools—later referred to as post-secondary for-profit universities. DeVry, which dates back to 1931, was known at the time as DeVry Institute of Technology. ITT Technology Initiative (later known as ITT Education Services) was founded in 1969. The vast University of Phoenix was created by John Sperling in 1976. Another one of the early players in the education industry was Joe Calihan, owner and operator of Bradford Proprietary Schools, which he founded in 1997.

THE SERVICES SECTOR

Some of the early important service providers were also established in the 1980s. Two of those companies receiving the bulk of funding were Sylvan Learning Systems, in which Saugatuck Capital invested in the first stage funding in 1986, and Bright Horizons, also founded in 1986, which was the first company to provide corporate-sponsored childcare. Other high profile service companies such as Kaplan and Aspen Youth Services received significant outside investor funding during the late 1980s as well.

Kaplan was originally founded in 1938 by Stanley Kaplan and was acquired by the Washington Post in 1977. Aspen Education Group was founded by Elliot Sainer in 1998 and was originally named Aspen Youth Services. The company is the leading provider of therapeutic health and educational services. Aspen's original business model was primarily driven by governmental special education funds, but later changed to a private pay model, which flourished. Aspen was purchased by CRC Health Group in 2006. Another significant player in the tutoring and supplemental services was Huntington Learning Centers, founded by Ray and Eileen Huntington As pioneers in the for-profit education industry, the Huntingtons opened their first learning center in 1977, with the goal of offering students professional tutoring to improve their learning skills. They have grown their business to more than 350 Huntington Learning Centers in over forty states. Most of these companies were grown organically over time, reducing the amount of outside capital needed.

THE PRODUCTS SECTOR

The products sector dates back to the 1800s. The J. L. Hammett Company was founded in 1862 as a school-supply company and is credited for inventing the chalkboard eraser as well as classroom slates. In addition to school supplies, this sector also included supplemental publishers such as Steck Vaughn Publishing, which was one of the original supplemental publishers, founded in 1936. These companies were considered among the earliest players in supplemental education.

The real leaders of the educational products sector, however, were the publishers. Investors are always looking for the next big opportunity, and the discovery of the little noticed industry of education publishing whet their appetites. Education publishing was especially attractive because there were already several large, profitable companies with proven track records. Surveying some of the significant financial transactions that were already taking place in the publishing arena during the mid-1990s can help explain Eduventures' optimism at that time about the potential for growth in the industry as a whole. Big players were getting into the game and there was lots of money changing hands as companies were staking claims in the education space.

Tracing the impact of publishers as it related to the education industry was an extremely significant challenge, as many of them had financial holdings in sectors other than in education. It was difficult to track them as a pure education company, and their businesses were complex and actively expanding. This sector was thought of as the "800-pound gorilla," and our coverage of these companies was more diversified than it was for other pure education companies. In reality, education was a small portion of the business for many of them. Also, Wall Street covered publishers as part of the media industry. Eduventures did, however, cover a few of the major publishers, including Houghton Mifflin, Pearson, McGraw Hill, Riverdeep, Scholastic, and Thomson (now known as Cengage Learning). The combined revenue for these companies in 2007 was approximately $20 billion. There was significant consolidation and merger and acquisition activity in education publishing in the 1990s and into the first decade of the 21st century. It is plausible that there was probably greater transaction activity in the ten-year period before 2001 than in centuries before, as publishers on the whole had generally been considered staid and somewhat staid businesses in terms of mergers and acquisitions.

Houghton Mifflin traces its roots back to 1832 in Boston and was originally a partner of Riverside Press. In 2001, it was acquired by French media giant Vivendi Universal for $5 billion. In 2002, facing mounting financial and legal pressures, Vivendi sold Houghton Mifflin to Thomas H. Lee Partners, Bain Capital, and the Blackstone Group at a loss of approximately $500 million. There was a significant interest in the acquisition of Houghton Mifflin, and many of the leading private equity firms bid on the transaction. They all had a strong interest because it was a premier brand and market leader, and its revenues had a great degree of predictability because of its consistent renewal contracts and adoptions by school districts. The predictability of revenues and the attractiveness of low-cost funding on favorable terms kept the blue chip private equity firms interested as they saw this as a very good opportunity.

An investor at Houghton Mifflin during this time has an interesting adage: the only thing better than buying a company is selling it at a profit. In December 2006, Houghton Mifflin was sold again, this time to Riverdeep, which was then and is still headed by former investment banker Barry O'Callaghan. O'Callaghan had assembled an impressive group of educational supplemental publishers through acquisition since 1999, including education brands such as Edmark, The Learning Company, and Broderbund. Riverdeep was able to finance the Houghton Mifflin deal by paying $1.75 billion in cash and assuming $1.61 billion in debt. The new enterprise was to be called Houghton Mifflin Riverdeep Group.

Following the acquisition of Houghton Mifflin, Riverdeep engaged in its second massive acquisition in July 2007. Houghton Mifflin Riverdeep Group purchased Harcourt Education, a division of Reed Elsevier, for $4 billion. A premier brand in education, Harcourt publishes textbook and supplemental materials and produces online materials. Harcourt's revenue at that time was $1.1 billion. The combination of Harcourt and Houghton Mifflin Riverdeep Group catapulted the conglomerate to a $3 billion company. Again, these transactions were facilitated during the giddy days of low interest rates and favorable financing terms, which featured little or no financial requirements from the buyers. In 2009, the days of easy credit ended, and Riverdeep restructured the $7 billion of debt, bracing for a challenging economic climate.

Another series of high finance transactions occurred as a result of the decision by Thomson to shed its education interests as a result of its merger with Reuters, the famed information and news company. This was a strategic decision to focus exclusively on individual markets that Thomson shared with Reuters. Thomson Corporation, which was one of the largest newspaper publishers in Canada and the United Kingdom, sold Thomson Learning Division to Apax Partners and OMERS Capital Partners in May 2007 in a deal valued at $7.75 billion. Apax Partners, based in London, is one of the oldest and largest private equity firms in the world, with approximately $30 billion under global management. OMERS Capital Partners is a private equity investment arm of the Ontario Municipal Employees Retirement System, one of Canada's largest pension funds. When Thomson Corporation announced its intention to sell Thomson Learning Group back in late October 2006, rumors circulated that the estimated price would run about $5 billion to $6 billion. The $7.75 billion sale amounted to 3.2 times the company's 2006 revenue of $2.4 billion with a profit of $383 million. Bidders for the division reportedly included other private-equity firms such as Kohlberg Kravis Roberts & Co., The Carlyle Group, and Warburg Pincus.

The interest of the buyers was attributable to a rare opportunity to purchase a large scalable company with significant potential for growth. Apparently, the competition was sufficient to run up the price. Along with the change of ownership for Thomson Learning came a new company name, Cengage Learning. The sale of its Learning Division added liquidity, allowing Thomson Corporation to complete the purchase of Reuters and form Thomson Reuters, a prominent global company.

McGraw Hill Education is a division of McGraw Hill Companies founded in 1888. The McGraw Hill Companies is a global information service provider serving the financial services, education, and business information markets. McGraw Hill Education covers virtually every aspect of the education market from pre-K through professional learning. They provide textbooks material, online learning, and multimedia tools and are one of the leading providers of reference and trade publishing. In 2000, McGraw Hill Companies purchased Tribune Education, a leading publisher of supplementary educational material for the K-12 markets. This acquisition fit well with McGraw Hill's Education division and helped solidify their position as the nation's largest provider of K-12 educational materials. McGraw Hill, like most publishers, dabbled in the dot-com boom by creating McGraw Hill Learning Network as a separate online division. Like other publishers who experimented with Internet ventures, they were unable to leverage its technology.

Pearson Education traces its origins back to 1725 when Thomas Longman published the first book typeset by Benjamin Franklin. Their Scott Foresman imprint, dating to 1889, helped generations of Americans learn to read with the first Dick, Jane, and Spot stories. In 1998, the emergence of Pearson Education as a world leader in the education industry occurred when the Viacom Corporation disposed of its major publishing assets. Addison-Wesley Longman and the educational businesses of Simon and Schuster joined Pearson Corporation and assisted in the creation of Pearson Education. Today, Pearson Education leads every major sector of educational publishing, including elementary and secondary school, higher education, professional education, English-language teaching, and educational technology, both in the U.S and internationally. They currently have over 100 education brands.

Some of these transactions proved winners. In 2000, Pearson acquired Dorling Kindersley, a reference publisher, and integrated it with Penguin to form Penguin Group. Another landmark moment in 2000 changed the world of education testing and assessment, with Pearson's $2.4 billion acquisition of National Computer Systems (NCS), which at the time was the leading educational testing and data management company in the United States. It would be the first such combination of a traditional publisher combining with education testing and data management. In the big picture of major global finance, these transactions were small investments compared to other blockbuster acquisitions.

Scholastic, the largest publisher and distributor of children's books (not just Harry Potter) and a leader in educational technology and children's media, rounded out the "big six." The company is grounded in scientific research and develops technology products and services that include intervention, instruction, assessment, professional development, and data management. Scholastic owns QED which was established in 1981. QED provides comprehensive marketing for the K-12 and higher education markets, including a comprehensive mailing list, data analysis, and market research.

From a business perspective, the transactions and stories regarding the publishers were among the most exciting in the early years of Eduventures' efforts to track the education industry. But it was clear that in many ways, education publishing was its own industry and was content to remain that way, despite having a major education focus and footprint. In terms of transformative potential, education publishing also turned out to be more conservative than reformist. Their investments in textbooks and print material remained so entrenched that it could be decades before they adapt to modern learning technologies afforded by the Internet. Education publishers have also faced a quandary as their customers (school districts) are strongly supported by teachers' unions, and backing any ventures which the unions opposed is always a challenge.

A whole new category was also emerging as a newly-minted sector of education called e-training and e-learning, but in reality, most of the training related to government, IT, and corporate training. Corporate training companies could have been funded through a variety of investors other than those following the educational sectors. The training and e-learning markets were blurred, whereas childcare, K-12, and post-secondary markets were well-defined. Clearly, the K-12 and post-secondary statistics could be pegged to GDP expenditures in K-12 and higher education numbers, and the numbers tracked by the Department of Education and federal government validated this. Today, most investment firms cover education based on K-12 and higher education and cover only a limited number of educational training companies.

HIGHER EDUCATION

Higher education is an easier sector to analyze as it is clearly distinct from K-12. Higher education companies are among the most successful education companies, and the for-profit companies in particular,` have permanently changed the ivory tower images of colleges and universities, and what a typical college student looks like. While not all investments in post-secondary education have been successes, higher education was clearly the most successful sector of the education market in the 1990s and was able to remain that way after the dot-com bust.

Some of the early success stories involved companies which provided course management systems such as Blackboard, founded in 1998, and Web CT. These companies offered tools which provided educators with Web-based teaching and learning platforms, as well as online course management tools.

In 2005, Blackboard acquired Web CT, at the time its top competitor, for $180 million. Blackboard made significant returns for its early investors who included The Carlyle Group, Frank Bonsal (co-founder of New Enterprise Associates), Novak-Biddle Venture Partners, and Bill Brock, former Tennessee senator and U.S. Secretary of Labor in the 1980s. These investors represented a new group who believed that the post-secondary markets reaped better returns than the K-12 markets.

Another of the important players in higher education was e-College, founded in 1996 as a company which could design an online learning platform specifically tailored for schools based on their needs. In 2007, e-College was sold to Pearson for $538 million, immediately making it one of Pearson's strategic assets. Capella is a strictly online university with approximately 24,000 students and a market value (in the fall of 2008) of over $800 million. Some of its original investors included ForstmannLittle, Cherry Tree Investments, and National Computer Systems. Also, Strayer Education, which was founded in 1892 as Strayer's Business College, experienced steady expansion for the next century, and then rode the post-secondary for-profit wave of the 1990s, going public in 1996 as Strayer Education, Inc. Strayer has enjoyed exceptional financial performance, and its market value is approximately $2.5 billion. In contrast to the K-12 sector, converting to online learning models proved to be a beneficial strategy for the for-profit universities.

Recent new players include American Public Education, which provides post-secondary education primarily to military and public service personnel in over 100 countries, was created through a combination of several post-secondary schools. This rollup was originally funded by William Blair for $100 million and has a present market value of approximately $850 million and an enrollment of over 33,000.

2009 continued to be prolific for the for-profit higher education companies with Grand Canyon Education going public in November 2008. In April 2009, Bridgepoint education completed its initial public offering with Warburg Pincus, and Michael Clifford sold some of their founding shares. In June 2009, Clifford announced another major deal in which he convinced a former General Electric chief executive officer, Jack Welch, to invest $2 million for a 12 percent stake in Chancellor University System LLC. Chancellor University will name its MBA program the Jack Welch Institute. In addition, Education Management Corporation (EDMC) completed a successful IPO after being taken private in 2006 by Providence Equity Partners, Goldman Sachs and Leeds Equity.

Although investors flocked to the flourishing post-secondary market, there were notable write-offs, including Fathom, Not Harvard.Com, Quisic, and Varsity Books. Even sophisticated investors such as Herb Allen of Allen and Company got involved in the post-secondary space. Allen invested $10 million in Global Education, whose mission was to provide the most comprehensive online liberal arts education to adults.

Fathom was founded in 2000 by Anne Kirshner, who had a successful record in Internet ventures, including the launch of NFL.com. The main backer was Morningside Ventures, Columbia University's for-profit Internet incubator. Six of the world's leading educational and cultural institutions partnered with Fathom to create what they hoped would be the premier site for knowledge and education on the Web. The founding partners included Columbia University, The London School of Economics, Cambridge University Press, The British Library, Smithsonian Institution National Museum of Natural History, and The New York Public Library. If prestige could create a winning company, Fathom had it, as well as incredible content and over $100 million invested. Unfortunately, Fathom was unable to execute and failed as they were unable to garner a customer base.

K-12 SCHOOLS

Throughout most of the 1990s, Eduventures' analysis continued to focus on the three original categories of K-12 schools, services, and products. The growth of the school category was enhanced as new legislation was enacted, giving schools more freedom to contract with private providers and bypass traditional union barriers. Existing private for-profit proprietary schools expanded, such as Challenger Schools, which started as a single preschool in San Jose, California in 1963 by school teacher Barbara Baker, and Fairmont Schools, founded in 1953 in Orange County, California, by Ken Holt, another former public school educator. These schools originated in the West, as there tended to be more openness and willingness for experimentation in that region. Another factor contributing to their growth during the 1990s was that Challenger and Fairmont each had tuition based at the same price point as public school expenditures, which at that time were between $5,000–$6,000 per pupil. This was substantially less than the elite not-for-profit private schools that dominate private K-12 offerings on the East Coast.

GOVERNMENT MOVES TO THE CHARTERS

In 1991, the first charter school legislation was passed in Minnesota, leading to a whole new movement of education reforms, including for-profit companies launching charter school programs. Minnesota has always had a rich civic culture and had been politically progressive in education reform. A very vibrant and well-organized business community there took a lot of civic pride in education and became a driving force for the legislative innovations that ushered in charter schools. Minnesota was a model for other states whose leaders were seeking charter school certification.

The most notable of all the for-profit charter schools was Edison Schools, founded by Christopher Whittle in 1992. When most people thought of "for-profit education" at the time, Edison was what typically came to mind, largely due to Whittle's high-profile public relations efforts. His original mission was to form a chain of private charter schools, but Edison was ultimately reinvented as a professional management company of public schools. Much of Whittle's vision traced back to the George H. W. Bush administration and his interaction with Lamar Alexander and David Kearns in the formation of New American Schools. Whittle had been at the table during that important time in education reform history as an advocate for a chain of for-profit charter schools. NAS's leadership listened, as at that time everything was deemed possible and, at a minimum, worth listening to.

In 1992, Bill Clinton defeated George H. W. Bush and the momentum of innovative, experimentation in education reform was palpable. While Bush wanted to be remembered as the "education president," it was Clinton who will be remembered as being the biggest supporter of experimentation in education for his support of the charter school movement. As a former governor, Clinton inspired other governors (ironically, mostly Republicans) to get involved in education reform, and many sponsored the early stages of the charter school movement, following in Minnesota's footsteps.

The crop of governors in the early to mid-1990s were truly passionate and committed education reformers. Education reform was at that time largely a bipartisan effort, and the governors were both leaders and doers, working diligently to pass the legislation to establish charter schools. Some of the governors who paved the way were John Engler (Michigan), Bill Weld (Massachusetts), Tommy Thomson (Wisconsin), Arne Corbin (Minnesota), Christine Todd Whitman (New Jersey), Tom Carper (Delaware), and Pete Wilson (California). Later to the cause came Jeb Bush (Florida), George W. Bush (Texas), and George Pataki (New York). These governors were outstanding in terms of their leadership and true passion for education reform. They made charter school legislation a top priority. In many ways, the torch that inspired then, while still burning, is today not as bright or united. It was a moment in time that needs to be rekindled for lasting education reform in America.

With education entrepreneurs helping to create legal space for innovation through legislation, names of for-profit charter school operators such as

Sabis, Edison, Advantage Schools, National Heritage, and Chancellor Beacon suddenly became the darlings of venture capitalists looking to support K-12 education reform. Over $1 billion was invested in these companies and other for-profit charters in the early and mid-1990s. Edison was the largest recipient, with over $232 million, and their history tells the story of the K-12 investment and political climate in microcosm.

To venture capitalists seeking scalable models in any young industry, shareholder liquidity is elusive. Edison believed that the only way to create liquidity for its shareholders was to go public, and they did just that in 1997 without ever showing a profit. The story of Edison and its IPO was an important milestone in the history of the emergence of the education industry. Their IPO in 1997 was covered by all the business and education media.

The IPO came on the heels of a previous stock offering by the Education Alternatives company in 1991. The CEO, John Golle, and his company had meteoric success and then a significant downturn. EAI had been known for its "Tesseract" method, built around customized instruction meant to prevent children from "falling through the cracks," and operated for-profit private schools. Education Alternatives had contracts to run public schools in Dade County, Florida, and later the failing school systems in Baltimore, Maryland, and Hartford, Connecticut. For the for-profit followers, Education Alternative represented a big hope for privatization as a means of education reform.

When Edison went public at $34 per share ($400 million market capitalization), it caught the attention of both Wall Street and the education community. Edison saw their valuation skyrocket to over $1 billion. The unions, however, were not receptive to a flamboyant entrepreneur with lots of promises and little measurable results. This put more pressure on Edison, and the more pressure they felt, the more they underperformed. Edison racked up operating losses in 1998 and 1999 of several hundred million. Then, in 2000, they reported a profit of $36 million, only to have that restated as the result of an investigation by a Securities and Exchange Commission that almost drove them into bankruptcy. The investigation focused on their practice of accounting for monies received from state and federal government which they booked as gross revenues. The results of the accounting review led to a restatement of the numbers that reflected a loss rather than a profit. Edison faced a crisis of survival; they urgently needed to find a partner to take them back to being a private company or file for bankruptcy.

One of the most interesting anecdotes from that time was when Chris Whittle explained that in that order to deal with the negative public image of "making money off the backs off children" and his need for school support, he decided to reduce Edison's profit objectives (despite the fact that they never made a profit) to a single digit number. In other words, a profit margin of 10 percent or higher was politically unacceptable, whereas a margin of 9 percent or less was, from a political standpoint, more acceptable. This decision was not a capitalist's mission to optimize profits, but rather a Faustian bargain to make peace with the unions and other detractors. At that time, it was clear that Edison was probably doomed as a public company because the discipline and promise of the free market had fallen under the political pressures.

While Edison never achieved its financial objectives, they ultimately did sell the company in a private transaction at $1.74 per share ($132 million) to Liberty Partners, a private investment company. To his credit, Whittle has stayed involved with Edison to this day. The company has adjusted their model and reinvented their vision and strategy as a professional management company of public schools The company has entered numerous public and private partnerships with schools and other not-for profit entities. Chris also invested his own personal funds into the Liberty Partners deal, so he too had "skin in the game." Ironically, at the time of the purchase, Liberty Partners was the manager of Florida's state education pension fund, and the funds invested for Edison came from a fund which contained public school teacher's retirement funds, making the deal quite controversial.

Many of the other charter school chains plotted a quieter course than Edison, and several have posted respectable financial and educational results. Nevertheless, in light of Edison's struggles to survive the difficult political climate around for-profit K-12 education, and to provide shareholder value as a publicly held company, most for-profit charter school companies have remained privately held. Because these companies are controlled by private individuals or small family investment funds, they have less external pressure from outside shareholders for liquidity events. The dream of large, publicly held for-profit school management chains, for the moment and maybe for decades, is on the back burner.

The Education Alternatives and Edison stories truly exemplified some of the boom-and-bust stories of private sector companies' management of K-12 public schools. Despite the enormous investment, Edison has never been able to achieve scale, which is always one of the biggest challenges in the K-12 school sector. While the political and legislative climate created enormous interest and possibilities in charter schools, local political challenges, particularly the unions and the educators' skepticism, proved too great for Edison and Education Alternative, alike. In addition, there was a need to constantly fight the perception of "making money off the backs of children," which has remained a significant barrier for creating a scalable business in the K-12 schools space.

THE KNOWLEDGE ECONOMY

In May 2000, Merrill Lynch published an important research report, *The Knowledge Web* by Michael Moe and Henry Blodget, that caught people's imagination about the possibility of a kids' market in technology and what some have called "edutainment." The thesis behind the kids' market and its relationship to the K-12 education market was based on data gathered by Merrill Lynch showing that online usage by kids and teens was growing by 33 percent per year. By 1998, 8.4 million kids were online, more than tripling the previous year's numbers. The forecast was that by 2003, 56 percent of all kids would be online. For teens, they stated "that while just under 20% of the teen population was online in 1997, we expect 18.5 million teens, or 72% to be online by 2003 at a growth of more than 25%." In fact, the *Knowledge Web* estimates were not only prescient, but actually quite conservative. While they did consider the social networking sites with a focus on young consumers, they did not anticipate the huge impact of social networking as a separate market as opposed to education.

Several hundred million dollars chased opportunities in the kids' market during this time. Companies such as Big Chalk, JuniorNet, MaMa Media, ZapMe, Classroom Connect, and High Wired tried to find ways to build bridges from the Internet into classrooms. High Wired, for example, sought to provide free Web publishing tools for high school students, classrooms, guidance offices, sports teams, and school newspapers.

The excitement around these efforts was palpable, and the prospects for an emerging K-12 online market looked very appealing on paper. Merrill Lynch has sized the overall addressable market at $357 billion and the for-profit business revenues at $1.3 billion, with a growth rate of 52 percent. It soon became clear, however, that the potential could not be realized. One of the under pinnings of the entire Merrill Lynch report was that these initiatives would help shape a new learning and education market with tremendous scalability because of the technology behind it. The entrenched education market was not ready or receptive. In fact, this was really a consumer market, and, unfortunately, the customers were not students. One of the reasons they were unsuccessful was because they were unable to generate broad appeal from the schools and teachers themselves, which is the lynchpin of scalability for the K-12 education market.

While the charter school movement saw opportunity through much of the 1990s, an even bigger phenomenon was fueling the growth of the education industry during that time—the Internet. The thesis of *The Knowledge Web* was centered on technology as the driver of the new economy. The report began:

> When the puck goes into the net, all sticks go in the air. Likewise, attributing what or who deserves the credit for the incredible economic boom we are experiencing is a crowded stage, Silicon Valley, Alan Greenspan, the fall of the Berlin Wall and, of course, the Internet are all leading actors amongst the cast of thousands in the New Economy script. Technology is the driver of the New Economy, and human capital is its fuel. In today's world, knowledge is making the difference not only in how well a country does. While the future possibilities of the knowledge economy look both exciting and, the same time, daunting, the transformation to a knowledge economy is now evident."

While their "knowledge economy" was broadly defined to include corporate, e-learning, and human capital management, the report singled out other opportunities in education. Their broad stroke estimated a $2 trillion market, catalyzed by the Internet e-learning and e-recruiting. E-learning and e-recruiting, the report said, was poised to revolutionize human capital management. Moe and Blodget defined human capital as a company's most important asset, its people, and thought that the Internet could make the staffing and human resource industries a $1 trillion market.

> Most striking is the dramatic pay gap between those with education and those without has more than doubled in less than 20 years. Looked at another way, the purchasing power of a 30-year-old man with a high -school diploma has dropped by over one-third over the past two decades."[1]

The report was chock-full of many exciting predictions, but the one that got Eduventures' attention was from John Chambers, CEO of Cisco Systems, who stated that "the next killer application for the Internet is going to be education." In many ways Moe and Blodget were viewed as being overly optimistic, but in looking back, that was not the case. Other forecasts were even actually conservative, such as the higher education online market forecast of $7 billion for 2003.

Here are some highlights of their financial forecasts.

Starting in 1999, the gold rush was on. Capital was like oxygen. Companies began breathing in cash and spending it just as fast in pursuit of an Internet jackpot. The excitement spilled over into non-Internet offerings as well. Whether well-managed or not, organizations in the education industry began catching the eye of venture capitalists. Entrepreneurs were focused on Internet services and education reform. Eduventures' data shows the total amount of investments made in 1999 was $2.6 billion and in the year 2000, $2.9 billion. That two-year total was more than all our combined previous coverage of investments in education. Though the numbers sounded enormous at the time, they paled in comparison to the total invested in all start-ups during the height of the Internet euphoria, where several hundred billion was invested in areas other than education.

This period also produced a whole new vocabulary: some of the new buzz words were vortals, portals, and hubs. The markets related to business were known as B2Bs (business to business) and consumers B2Cs (business to consumers). The only problem was that, due to the speed of market formulation, companies were categorizing themselves as one or the other without understanding exactly what markets they truly served.

At the peak of the education bubble around 2000, Eduventures' estimated that over two-thirds of the private investments made in education went toward Internet-based companies. Investors clearly believed the education industry offered a significant profit opportunity due to its large market size, ongoing technological transformation, and regulatory reforms, particularly the E-Rate program. Which provides discounts to assist school libraries to obtain affordable telecommunications.

At the same time, broadband providers were also investing strongly in education Internet ventures. Dell Computer pumped $28 million into Campus Pipeline; Media One spent the same amount on Classroom Connect. Sony, Microsoft, Liberty Media, and Comcast partnered to put $32 million into Lightspan. RCN invested $70 million in Junior Net, while Vulcan Ventures gambled big with a $100 million stake in Net Library. These numbers appeared to be in the stratosphere as education entrepreneurs at the time were only seeking an average of $1–$5 million.

THE VENTURE BOOM

Venture capital enthusiasm, for better or worse, fueled the companies of the Internet-era. In reality, business models around this time were all over the map—in a way that seemed to diverge from traditionally successful entrepreneurial booms. Initially, platform providers emerged with a wealth of resources for children, parents, and educators. Most investors had no idea what was going to work and what was utterly unrealistic. Many people were all caught up in an euphoric state, believing in hype and bombastic promises. Even the savviest of investors got caught in the middle and bought in. Ultimately, this boom would prove to be short-lived. Of approximately $6 billion invested in 1999 and 2000, approximately half of it was lost or written off by 2002. So what happened? Why did it happen? And what were the unintended consequences?

The Internet-boom has often been compared to the tulip mania in Holland during the Dutch's Golden Age, when prices for tulip bulbs sold for more than twenty times the annual income of a skilled craftsman. Education was a small piece of that overall phenomenon. The "knowledge economy," as defined by Moe and Blodget, may have represented the craze for Internet investments, but $6 billion of investments represented a small portion of our overall total economy. The challenge in some of the thinking at the time was that technology and human capital could entirely replace old brick and mortar enterprises. Like all successful entrepreneurs, they were a little ahead of their time. Investors were so enamored with this idea that there was little capital available for the still-needed brick and mortar investments (unless there was an e-learning or e-enterprise component).

The most significant consequence of the dot-com boom-and-bust resulted from the behavior of venture capitalists and their overzealous desire to put their money to work without proper due diligence. Some of the greatest names and investors in U.S. history were participants in this lemming-like behavior during the speculative bubble. So much so, that high profile investors such as Vulcan Ventures (founded by Microsoft co-founder Paul Allen), Kohlberg Kravis Roberts, Charles River Ventures, Kleiner Perkins, and Forstmann Little indirectly persuaded other smaller investors to participate in the boom, without doing the appropriate due diligence with an eye towards bust.

Private equity firms such as Leeds Capital, Warburg Pincus, and industry specific funds like Quad Ventures have stayed the course on education. Strategic investors Sterling Capital (formerly Sylvan Ventures), Kaplan, Knowledge Universe, and the major publishers remained involved based on their long-term commitment to education. These groups ultimately gained significant financial rewards for their patience. Other investors, such as Patricof & Co., Vulcan Ventures, GE Capital, and telecommunication and cable companies such as RCN, Liberty, Comcast, and AOL, were willing to take their write-offs, as they had hedged their capital and were in and out of education opportunistically.

The most disappointing aspect of this period was the lack of due diligence related not only to supporting unproven business models, but in raising unrealistic expectations. Investors exerted pressure on the heads of the companies, who in many cases were former educators or first-time entrepreneurs with no operating experience. The early investors were generous in investing their cash and then suddenly demanded performance from CEOs whose financial skill sets or experience had not been properly vetted from the beginning. The unforeseen and unintended consequence of this period was that the vast majorities of the investors were not aware of or never acknowledged their mistakes, meaning that a young industry, which needed more entrepreneurial experience and more investor experience on the whole, lost important opportunities to learn.

Typically, venture capital investors are those who will take the time to mentor start-ups and help them grow into the opportunities that the visionary entrepreneurs foresaw. But the dot-com boom-and-bust resulted in a glut of investors who followed nebulous and previously unmeasured data, such as clicks and hits in pursuit of the promised rewards of portals. After writing off their losses, many venture fund operators decided to reinvent themselves as private equity firms. Originally, private equity was defined as an investment firm dealing with mature companies, and venture capital with early stage ventures. Burned by their opportunistic investment failures, many venture capitalists turned very conservative and considered investing only in companies with proven business models. With proven business models, they wanted a private equity stake. Unfortunately, the result was that most capable education entrepreneurs did not meet this new criterion, and the private capital so desperately needed for innovation in K-12 schooling dried up.

The people who ended up paying the price for these errors in judgment were education entrepreneurs. As these entrepreneurs continued to seek out new investors, they suddenly were faced with new criteria and rigid guidelines, such as a minimum of $10 million in revenues, three years of operating profits (EBITDA), an experienced, proven management team, and consistent growth with a sustainable business model. Venture capitalists began to resemble banks who were only willing to loan small businesses money when they didn't need it. Emergent education entrepreneurs who had solid business models and far more experience than their predecessors, found very few ways for funding their dreams and plans. This was disheartening to everyone, as there were many entrepreneurs struggling for funding who had business models far superior to some of the junk that had been previously funded during the dot-com intoxication.

Nearly $6 billion was invested in education between 1999 and 2000, and approximately half of it was lost. Maybe it was not such a big deal in the overall investment world, but for education—an emerging industry sector that was trying to find a coherent definition and a trustworthy identity—it was a significant loss. A lot of big money investors had jumped on the bandwagon, dabbled, lost money, and moved on, leaving the sector with little access to cash. According to the Venture Capital Association's data, education represented approximately 3 percent of total venture capital investments in the that period. Total investments in the dot-com boom were in the range of $300 billion, so the $6 billion invested in education seemed insignificant. The dot-com bust as a whole looks like small potatoes compared to the real estate subprime loans and credit market losses that catapulted into the trillions almost a decade later.

Ultimately, the 1990s resulted in the clear differentiation between the K-12 and post-secondary education markets in terms of investment criteria and priorities. Despite strong interest in K-12, approximately 70 percent of all investment activity shifted to the post-secondary market in the first decade of the 21st century—nearly the complete opposite of the environment in the early 1990s. Though K-12 is a larger market (almost twice the size of post-secondary), the failure of the charter schools to create scale quickly enough, combined with heavy continuing resistance from the teachers' unions and continuing skepticism from educators themselves, set the stage for a diminished interest by the investment community. The fizzle for K-12 was the failure of high-profit venture capital investments to reach the largest and fastest growing market of the Internet—children. The higher education market, by contrast, proved more receptive to investments in new learning technologies, particularly online.

THE VENTURE BUST

For the education industry, the bust ushered in a new, harsher reality. In March 2001, Eduventures did a retrospective on 1990–2000 called *Venture Capitalists Seek Reality, Revenues and Rational Business Models.* The gist of the report was that 2000 was a year of reversals, adjustment, and learning for entrepreneurs and venture capitalists in the education economy. Our introduction read: "As the roaring bull market of the 1990s came to an end and the bear market of 2000 took hold, those who banked on innovation and risk-taking found themselves exposed to the Darwinian side of market-driven economic forces."

Eduventures interviewed some leading educational investors from that time about the future of their companies and the education market. Many remained committed to education; others opted to bow out gracefully and indicated they were going to leave the education market and focus on the training market (though many viewed this as a lateral sort of move because of training's relation to education). In particular, conversations with Christopher Hoehn-Saric (chairman and CEO, Sylvan Ventures), Deborah Devedjian (vice president, Education & Training Investments, Warburg Pincus), Elliot Royce (senior vice president, GE Equity), and George Jenkins (general partner, Patricof & Co. Ventures, Inc.) shed light on the learning process and the realignments that took place at that time.

Eduventures: "Can you assess the current state of venture capital activity in education?"

Hoehn-Saric, Sylvan Ventures: "The market has definitely contracted from
the perspective of availability of capital. However, institutional investors
(e.g., publishers) are continuing to invest in this area. A few years ago, a
number of institutional investors were aware of opportunities in this area
but were less aware of [investment] issues such as valuation.

"We've also seen a pullback in the funding of niche opportunities. A
few years ago, people thought they could enter markets [e.g., K-12,
post-secondary, etc.] with any asset and move into other adjacent areas. Now, we're seeing that potential investments have to be the right
opportunities. The most important criteria right now is, "Is the opportunity
scalable?""

Devedjian, Warburg Pincus: "We're in "back to basics" mode. The venture
capital community is reviewing, digesting and regurgitating its current
portfolios. A few years ago, many investors got overexcited about online
and technology companies, but they failed to ask the tough questions about
business fundamentals. Now, we're back to what venture capital investing
has been about historically—a deep knowledge of the marketplace that
enables funds to invest in serious management teams with proprietary technologies, assets or customer or vendor relationships; realistic financials;
and potential for significant financial gains."

Jenkins, Patricof & Co.: "We remain confident that our thesis is right—training and education is one of the more clear-cut uses of the Internet. As
a firm, we've committed a significant amount of money to training and
education investments and we will continue to make investments and be
opportunistic in 2001. However, it is still an area in which investors need
to be patient."

Royce, GE Equity: "From a stock price perspective, it's been a difficult
year. However, look at the underlying business fundamentals of leading
e-learning companies such as Docent and DigitalThink and you'll see
that leading e-learning companies are actually exceeding expectations.
Far too many people focus too closely on short-term movements of stock
prices."

This period accelerated the much-needed mutual-learning curve between
Wall Street and the environment of schools on Main Street. Christopher
Hoehn-Saric's observations reflected the ways in which entrepreneurs and
investors were beginning to understand how schools really operated. While
there may have been new computers in the classrooms, school district
central offices had not advanced the way other professional service offices
had. People from earlier generations always marvel at how schools and
classrooms look the same as when they attended, while other professional

offices, whether they are accounting, legal, or medical, look very different today.

The inability of local school districts to convert to modern technology had a significant negative impact on school supply companies attempting to modernize their distribution systems. Businesses such as JuneBox.com, which was founded by School Specialty, and J. L. Hammett Company's Ezone product never got off the ground, as the customer was not ready to adapt. School districts to this day have been slow to keep pace with other business e-procurement activities.

The technological illiteracy of school districts contributed to the significant write-off of investments in what were called "Education Hubs." According to Merrill Lynch, in *The Next Online Land Grab for E-portals & Hubs,* "Forty–two million kids and teens online at home, not to mention their parents, by 2003 clearly make the home e-education market attractive. The school market is equally compelling, covering 53 million school children and 3 million teachers."

Major portals did emerge in K-12 and higher education, but few claimed the territory that Merrill Lynch had mapped out for them.

In retrospect, the hope at Eduventures to be present at the birth and help facilitate the quick maturation of a viable education industry was unrealistic. At the time of the dot-com boom, though, the excitement in the air was palpable, and our forecasts reflected this general mood of optimism. After the dust settled from the dot-com bust the investment landscape had changed. The resulting lack of access to capital for early stage for-profit ventures in K-12 resulted in a policy and market shift towards not-for-profits. Unfortunately, the dream of a fully integrated K-12 through post-secondary for-profit education industry has yet to be realized. A bifurcation took place between the K-12 and Higher education markets in terms of investor groups. K-12 was primarily supported by not-for-profits and newly established foundations while higher-education was the darling of the private investment community.

Many in the investment community also shifted their focus to higher education because the political climate was more favorable than K-12. Not only was higher education largely immune from the criticisms of for-profit education being sustained by the teachers' unions and other education groups, but there were easier ways to capture part of the federal funding streams that were available through student loans. While the student loan market has experienced its own boom-and-bust, for-profit higher education continues to grow.

The remnants of the K-12 for-profit market shrunk in terms of a profitable market, with the exception of the tutoring and testing market and the business opportunities created through the No Child Left Behind Legislation, which created a separate industry sector for Supplemental Education Suppliers (SES). The sector-specific trade associations also followed a similar pattern of bifurcation, with the K-12 industry groups languishing while the higher education Career College Association becoming more viable, as higher-education for-profit leaders lobbied for the Higher Education Act of 2000.

The dot-com boom-and-bust taught us that both education-industry success and education reform require more forms of capital than merely money. After the dot-com bust, the baton of innovation in K-12 education effectively passed to the entrepreneurial foundations and social venture firms who continued to recognize that K-12 reform would require entrepreneurial innovation disciplined not only by market forces, but also by rigid accountability and widely accepted performance standards.

THE NEED FOR HUMAN CAPITAL

In the end, without the proper human capital, financial capital is wasted. The early education entrepreneurs had been exposed to pressures on all sides: political pressures from the teachers' unions and their allies, financial pressures from over-eager and under-committed investors, performance pressures from federal accountability regulations such as No Child Left Behind, and, finally, the pressures of passive resistance as school administrators proved unable or unwilling to adapt enthusiastically to the changes technology seemed to be foisting upon them.

The ultimate emergence of a viable K-12 education industry attracting vast public sector financial investment and political support will depend a great deal on how well the lessons of the past twenty years are taken to heart by both the investment and education reform communities. Even then there remains an intractable challenge. If K-12 is to realize the maximum benefits of private sector infusions of financial and human capital, there will have to be major political concessions by the teachers' unions and their allies, releasing their stranglehold on serious discussion of issues such as school choice, teacher merit pay, incentives, and an increase in the number of charter schools. While the momentum shifted among the venture capitalists from K-12 to higher education, there are still billions of dollars on the sidelines eager to get back in the K-12 market as well.

In many respects, the consequence of the boom-and-bust period resulted in a change of definition of the for-profit education investor. Private sector entrepreneurs such Bill Gates and Eli Broad have used the wealth they created to build philanthropic endeavors that would employ financial and human capital to transform education, particularly where it was most needed. The capital they created through their private sector activities was reinvested in new entities that included charter schools and public school programs. A decade later the playing field is being leveled again worldwide, and government is supporting the problem with an eye towards entrepreneurs who will and can make the greatest impact.

Chapter 8

Building Sustainable Structure
for the Education Industry

Chapter 8 reveals how a sustainable education industry emerged after the Internet boom-and-bust period. The chapter illustrates the balance of financial and human capital necessary for successful investment as new sources of funding evolved and industry infrastructure was built. Some examples of new funders covered in the chapter are the "new" venture philanthropist, corporate, foundation social entrepreneurs, and social venture capitalists. This chapter highlights some of the industry's post-boom infrastructure, which brought together likeminded people in industry trade associations, trade press, and industry advocacy groups for government relations. Finally, the chapter covers newly established foundations recognized for their important support for the charter school movement.

By 2005, in the wake of the dot-com bust, it seemed that the original hope for a rapidly maturing education industry supported by private sector investment and entrepreneurship would fall short. The sale of Eduventures provided me time to reflect on events of the previous decade and on the challenges of the K-12 market in general. Few for-profit companies in K-12 had seemed to achieve scale, profits, and returns for their shareholders. But it was apparent that there was still tremendous energy in this space.

In fact, it became clear that despite what seemed to be a drying up of private sector investment in education, the time for entrepreneurship in K-12 education had not passed, but was just getting started (albeit with new and different players). Slowly, but steadily over the preceding decade, a K-12 education industry had indeed been emerging, anchored by new partnerships between philanthropists and charter school entrepreneurs. This industry, though not what we originally envisioned, was strong, complete with diverse support services, including industry associations, lobbying firms, head hunters, research information, and public relations services.

After the sale of Eduventures, relocating to the West Coast to think through these questions was attractive, because while the K-12 market had been slow to broadly develop, it seemed that there was always significant innovation taking place in California. The West Coast also provided an environment that facilitated reflecting on the changing landscape of the education industry. One important industry player in Los Angeles is Gib Hentschke at the University of Southern California.

While Gib wears many hats as an education entrepreneur, his official title is the Richard T. Cooper and Mary Catherine Cooper chair in public administration in the USC Rossier School of Education. He had previously served as president of the Education Industry Association. With Gib's endorsement, the Rossier School of Education at the Univerity of Southern California offered me an opportunity to serve as the 2006–2007 Executive-in-Residence.

Executives-in-Residence generally share their own personal, professional experiences and observations with the graduate students and doctoral candidates in education and business. In 2006, the Executive-in-Residence opportunity allowed for reflection on industry trends over the past twenty years, as well as a chance to research capital flow for K-12 entrepreneurs, the roles of not-for-profit ventures in education, and their growth, performance, and trends for scale.

The academic environment at USC, with its proximity to philanthropic leaders with significant investment in education, shaped the study of recent years in education. The dot-com bust resulted in the creative destruction of the classic model of venture capital as related to education ventures. After the bust, many of the venture capitalists who had make a commitment to the education industry determined that there would be better returns if they invested in more mature companies. Unfortunately, the only investable mature businesses at the time were in higher education and in traditional publishing, so K-12 was largely left behind. Newly reminted as private equity firms, the herd of venture capitalists refocused their K-12 investment criteria, while existing private equity firms also sought to invest in the rapidly expanding higher education market. This begged the question of how education entrepreneurs in the K-12 space, going forward, were to seek out funding.

USC also offered proximity to another education industry laboratory at Stanford University (proximity, that is, when compared with coming from the East Coast!). There, Paul Kim, assistant dean and chief technology officer of Stanford University's School of Education, had recently become involved with a company in digital publishing called INETOO. With the participation of some students of the Stanford Graduate School of Education, INETOO was beta testing a learning platform that contextually integrated digital content with the latest Web 2.0 collaboration technologies. The platform also provided critical learning intelligence for universities and content providers based on user activity and content usage.

The founders of INETOO, Robert Brouwer and Ahmed Abdulwahab, are two education entrepreneurs from Europe who had developed the technology with the help of the TATA Software Company, in partnership with IBM Global Education. It's their belief the business platform would destroy the stranglehold that education publishers had enjoyed on the textbook market, both new and used.

WEST COAST ENERGY

The West Coast provided a very different business climate than Boston. Unlike Easterners, who are more cautious, West Coasters are very receptive to entrepreneurial ideas. It was exhilarating, and the "can do" atmosphere was felt everywhere. The willingness and openness to discuss new ideas of Californians was refreshing and motivating. They demonstrated how important it is to exchange success stories as a method to inspire support for entrepreneurial education reform.

With opportunities for ongoing industry research and networking, as well as time for reflection, California served as a wonderful base for two years. There, it was easy to make contacts and develop relationships with many education entrepreneurs because of the high number of innovators on the West Coast. In particular, Silicon Valley had long been considered an incubator for innovators and entrepreneurs. The area was revered for its forward-thinking venture capital community.

A SECOND LOOK AT A GROWING INDUSTRY

Looking more at the enterprise than at the investment level, it was clear that, despite the recent boom-and-bust of investing in the education industry, a whole new breed of successful education entrepreneurs had quietly emerged and was making a difference. The measurement of success for these entrepreneurs was not solely based on making money for the shareholders of their companies, but was also based on improving the educational opportunities and performance of students.

NEW INVESTORS

With the absence of venture capital investors in the K-12 sector, other sources of capital from outside firms such as Keiretsu (a Japanese word meaning a close group of closely held companies) became important. Keiretsu is a network of over 100 investors supporting entrepreneurs. Membership is by invitation only and is comprised of serious investors, venture capitalists, corporate CEO's, institutional investors, and serial entrepreneurs. Their relationships facilitate access to capital for early stage companies. Many invested beyond education but were open and receptive to meeting education entrepreneurs. One great benefit of the group is that a presenter from each company seeking money is video recorded while making his or her presentation, and the video is played back to the group's members for their constructive critique. It is a great opportunity for entrepreneurs to receive this type of first-hand feedback from investors in a constructive form that they can use for future endeavors.

Another investor was John Doerr, a famed Silicon Valley venture capitalist, who with the support of his partners at Kleiner Perkins Caulfield and Byers had successfully sponsored investments in highly regarded entrepreneurial companies such as Compaq, Amazon, Sun Microsystems, and Millenium Pharmaceutical. Building on his own experience, he chose to look for the same attributes in his philanthropic projects supporting educational entrepreneurs as he does in his investments. As he said in an article in *Time* magazine, "I like to see a passionate founding entrepreneur, strategic focus on large underserved need, scalability and the ability to become a freestanding venture." Doerr saw the need and opportunity in education and identified an ideal investment target in Kim Smith, an educational and social entrepreneur, who began her career as a consultant specializing in business-education partnerships.

In 1989, Kim had become a founding team member of Teach for America (TFA). Kim has a bachelor's degree in political science and psychology from Columbia College and a masters degree in business from Stanford. She was tapped by Doerr to develop and build NewSchools Ventures Fund (NewSchools) whose mission was to transform education by supporting education entrepreneurs.

Kim's model was to create a "hybrid" approach to investing in education. NewSchools uses grants, loans, and equity investments to support a portfolio of ventures in education, both not for-profit and for-profit. The key driver for NewSchools is their passion to support and encourage education entrepreneurs to create positive educational outcomes. These drivers have paid off over the past decade. NewSchools has strategically invested approximately

$100 million while achieving positive results measured not primarily by profit, but by student achievement and enterprise sustainability.

NewSchools has funded some of the most successful performance-oriented charter schools, including KIPP Academies, one of the leading charter school groups, and a not-for-profit corporation. NewSchools not only funds schools, but also seeks to develop educational leaders, while improving infrastructure and facilities. New Schools' work proves that developing metrics for performance beyond mere profits can stimulate some of the most interesting ventures in educational entrepreneurship today. NewSchools also sought out and collaborated with major foundations that have emerged as the pioneers of a newly defined education industry for the K-12 market.

In 2005, NewSchools Ventures strengthened its deep commitment to education by appointing Ted Mitchell as its CEO. Ted is known, nationally, as a highly regarded leader in education. He was recently president of Occidental College and was previously vice chancellor of UCLA and deputy to the president of Stanford University. In addition, Kim Smith remains as an active board member and senior advisor.

PHILANTHROPISTS

When capital resources were drying up, philanthropic investments from education entrepreneurs provided a sustaining force. From a historical perspective, the Carnegie Corporation was a forerunner of entrepreneurs using their fortunes to reinvest in education. Andrew Carnegie's efforts in education in the early 20th century were focused on supporting the teaching profession, both by supporting colleges of education and through promoting financial security for teachers through a retirement fund. Carnegie created the Teachers Insurance and Annuity Association of America, TIAA-CREF, which is now one of the world's largest insurance companies.

In recent years, under the leadership of its president, Dr. Vartan Gregorian, the Carnegie Corporation has focused on supporting the efforts of NewSchools Venture Fund and Teach For America because of their efforts to bring college students into K-12 classrooms. In many ways, Gregorian, whom people refer to with reverence as a true "Renaissance man," has quietly been an education entrepreneur. Formerly provost at the University of Pennsylvania, he was also the president of the New York City Public Library and administrator of the Annenberg Education Challenge.

Because of Eduventures' role in the marketplace, we were afforded some interesting consulting projects that acquainted us with emerging educational philanthropy. After the Gates family contributed $29 billion to their foundation, they had launched an ambitious global health initiative to prevent deadly diseases such as tuberculosis and AIDS in Africa and other poor regions. They then decided to expand to public education, where inequities in America had long troubled them. Since 2000, the Gates Foundation has invested over $1 billion in education, primarily focused on drop-out prevention in high schools.

Tom Vander Ark, a former school superintendent in Seattle, directed the Gates family's philanthropic endeavors in education until 2006. Exhibiting significant skills in public entrepreneurship, Tom worked with policymakers, persuading them of the urgency of addressing our significant high school drop out problem, which was reaching upwards of 30 percent. While the Gates Foundation has not yet seen significant results in reducing drop-out rates, they are making progress. Another cornerstone of their efforts is smaller class size. Working with visionary school district leaders such as Joel Klein (New York City), Arne Duncan (Chicago; now U.S. Secretary of Education), Paul Vallas (New Orleans), and Michelle Rhee (Washington DC), the Gates Foundation is educating and equipping those in the trenches. The effort and resources of the Gates Foundation have created tangible programs and fostered significant public and government engagement. A full-fledged education entrepreneur, Tom is now managing partner of a multistage private equity firm focused on education, Revolution Learning.

Kevin Hall, the education program officer for the Eli and Edythe Broad Foundation, was one of the many entrepreneurs who sought a career in the education industry. Prior to joining the Broad Foundation, he was involved in the management of Chancellor Beacon Academies, which was a major chain of for-profit schools based in Florida. Chancellor Beacon later sold to Dennis and Eileen Bakke and now operates under the name of Imagine Schools. Kevin knows the K-12 market well and has the battle scars to prove it. He and his boss, Dan Katzir, have built the Broad Foundation into a highly regarded education foundation with enormous influence and credibility in the education reform movement. Under the tutelage of Eli and Edythe Broad, they have focused on improving the management and governance of schools and their districts by providing training programs for superintendents and school board members.

The Pisces Foundation, founded by the late Donald and Doris Fisher, founders of the Gap stores, seeks to leverage significant private resources to spark change in public education. As supporters of charter schools, the Fishers were one of the original funders of the Center for Education Reform. The Pisces Foundation had also funded the Stratford Schools in California, which had been founded by Joe Wagner after his short stint with me at Eduventures. Joe ultimately sold the business to the education investor fund Quad Ventures. The Pisces Foundation also became the original investors in the Knowledge

Is Power Program (KIPP), supporting them early on. KIPP was founded in 1994 and at present operates thirty-eight schools in fifteen states. The Pisces Foundation offered start-up funding to help recruit principals and train them in launching the new schools.

Pisces also helped create the Pacific Charter Development Group, which helped fund other entrepreneurial ventures in education. They have partnered with NewSchools Venture Fund from time to time and coinvested with them in Aspire Public Schools, Green Dot Schools in Los Angeles, and others. They also invested in Teachscape and Teach For America. Pisces also helped catalyze partnerships among the Broad Foundation, Walton Foundation, and the Bill and Melinda Gates Foundation, creating a consortium of the most influential philanthropic venture funds for education in the United States.

The work of these foundations and many others is an important piece of the story about the future of educational entrepreneurship. In an industry where entrepreneurial energy has been more often frowned upon than encouraged, and where significant barriers to new entrants exist, philanthropic capital has proven to be an important tool for fostering innovation and entrepreneurship. These philanthropic initiatives and others like them will prove to have been effective and sustainable investors in the new K-12 education industry.

CHARTER SCHOOLS

Two other important figures in the California education market are Mitch Gordon and his good friend Mike Piscal. Mitch had founded a company called Lesson Lab, a K-12 professional development company, which was acquired in 2006 by Pearson Education and now is part of Pearson Achievement Solutions. Mike Piscal ran a number of charter schools in South Central Los Angeles under the umbrella organization Inner City Education Foundation.

Mike was running a charter school for high school students in the Crenshaw area of South Central. The school entrance had some fresh bullet holes, and you could see Crenshaw High School a block away. Mike had chosen that location deliberately, as Crenshaw was a famous high school in Los Angeles which had produced many professional sports athletes well known in Los Angeles. Sadly, however, Crenshaw High School had already had seven murders that year, including some gang-related drive-by shootings. Mike has a vision for changing the learning environment in LA's toughest neighbor-hoods, through goals, focus, and discipline, and some of the tactics related to team building in athletics.

In October 2008, just before the presidential elections, the *Wall Street Journal* wrote an editorial about how entrepreneurs can change education.

They wrote about the Inner City Education Foundation and its charter school network founded by Mike Piscal:

> With economic issues sucking up so much political oxygen this year, K-12 education hasn't received the attention it deserves from either Presidential candidate. The good news is that school reformers at the local level continue to push forward. This month the Inner City Education Foundation (ICEF), a charter school network in Los Angeles, announced plans to expand the number of public charter schools in the city's South Central section, which includes some of the most crime-ridden neighborhoods in the country. Over the next four years, the number of ICEF charters will grow to 35 from 13. Eventually, the schools will enroll one in four students in the community, including more than half of the high school students. The demand for more educational choice in predominantly minority South Los Angeles is pronounced. The waitlist for existing ICEF schools has at times exceeded 6,000 kids. And no wonder. Like KIPP, Green Dot and other charter school networks that aren't constrained by union rules on staffing and curriculum, ICEF has an excellent track record, particularly with black and Hispanic students."[1]

The article went on to point out that despite the success of ICEF, the California Teachers Association and its backers continued to oppose school choice and observed that other states, including New York, Ohio, Florida, Connecticut, Utah, and Arizona, face similar opposition. Mike Piscal's work is a motivator for all education entrepreneurs.

I had long thought that charter schools offered a simple and elegant model for school reform and had tracked their progress since meeting Jeannie Allen, the founder of the Center for Education Reform (CER). Since founding CER in 1995, Jeannie has tirelessly fought the battles against the teachers' unions and their political allies who want to see charters disappear. She is a passionate believer in the possibility of systemic education reform, and she has been fortunate to get financial support year after year. CER provides valuable data, research, and, most importantly, advocacy for the importance of charter schools and their role of providing options to parents and students. Jeannie's team produces state-by-state directories and reports analyzing each state's legislation and the leaders' positions and performance, all the while not sugar-coating her assessments. This sort of research has been and will continue to be an essential structural building block for the maturation of the charter school industry in particular and a K-12 education industry overall. The charter school movement is in its second decade of existence. The CER tracks charter school performance, which under any objective analysis outperforms public schools. CER's data speaks for itself, but human stories, such as Mike Piscal's, add a powerful, personal touch in making the political and business case for charters.

MEASURING CHARTER SCHOOL PERFORMANCE

Being at USC also offered the opportunity to observe first hand the work of Gib Hentschke and Penny Wohlstetter at USC's Center on Educational Governance (CEG), which provides another model for research and community engagement in education reform. CEG focuses on the linkage between policy, educational governance, and the improvement of urban schools and systems. Engaging faculty from across USC, including the Rossier School of Education, the Marshall School of Business, and the School of Policy, Planning, and Development, Center researchers use an interdisciplinary approach to study current policy solutions to the educational issues posed by diverse urban communities—local, national, and global. The main activities of the Center are: (1) engaging in rigorous quantitative and qualitative research studies of policy problems; (2) building a knowledge base to provide researchers, educators, parents, and policy makers with new tools and strategies for improvement; and, (3) working in partnership with educators and policy makers to use research to improve policy and practice. Current projects include U.S. and multi-national studies of school networks and strategic alliance, charter schools, leadership, data-driven decision making, and educational reform.

What was most interesting was CEG's work on charter school performance. As independently operated public schools that have considerable autonomy over their budgets, educational programs, and staffing, charter schools are expected to innovate and become lighthouses, spreading ideas for school improvement to other public schools. CEG researchers realized that charter schools were each developing metrics beyond test scores to measure performance of their schools, but that little sharing of innovative practices across schools was occurring.

The signature product of the CEG Advisory Board is the USC Compendium of Promising Practices, which identifies and documents strategies for improving school performance. "Promising Practices" are defined here as strategies of schools (not individual teachers) that are new or existing ideas that have not been widely disseminated. The term is employed to convey a sense of innovation and potential impact. The Compendium has three goals: (1) to provide evidence-based strategies for improving schools and student performances; (2) to inspire educators to replicate or adapt new strategies to improve school performance; and (3) to share new knowledge and expertise about what works to improve the whole public school system. The Center has also developed a searchable online database of innovative programs, policies, and processes used by charter schools throughout California.

As charter schools increasingly became a centerpiece of education reform, politics necessarily began to play a greater role because of the way our school systems are structured. Public support of for-profit charter schools has waxed and waned. Many states established charter school legislation. But under pressure from teachers' unions, some states were forced to change the legislative process for approval of charter schools to ensure that legislation would provide charters only to charter operation enterprises that were established as not-for-profit entities. Such legislation did not prohibit for-profit companies from agreeing to be subcontracted by the charter operator as such, but it prevented the expansion of charters from being issued to for-profit companies. The premise that private ventures could yield public good in the form of significant education reform and school improvement was under scrutiny.

Before the charter school idea fully flowered, the bud began falling off its rose shortly after the demise of Education Alternatives, John Golle's early and bold initiative in school management. Then came the high-profile disappointment of Edison's public stock offering. Whether it was fair for investors and the public at large to judge the prospects for an industry on two of its earliest endeavors, the Edison setback had enough of an emotional impact to kill serious interest in for-profit charters as an attractive investment vehicle for Wall Street and the public markets. The sentiment among investors, whether early stage investors or social venture funds, was that for-profit charter schools were not a scalable model and therefore would not provide adequate returns for their investors. For the record, Edison, to its credit, did redesign its model to work more in public/private partnership with the schools and school boards who became their clients. Investors were not willing to stay along for this learning process.

What was less visible to the public, however, was that the charter school movement did not go away but rather became the domain for a new breed of education entrepreneurs focused on supporting charter schools—typically utilizing not-for-profit organizations or privately held firms—while demanding accountability, performance, and tangible outcomes. These charter organizations worked quietly and diligently behind the scenes for years while the winds of education reform swirled around them.

THE SPECIAL EDUCATION MARKET

Despite the political challenges faced by for-profit companies and charter schools, significant policy changes and implementation of new ideas in education as a result of the growing focus on standards, performance, and accountability had potential to encourage education entrepreneurs. Government legislation, for example, impacted the alternative or special education market during the 1970s.

Access to free, quality education is the key to the uniquely American promise of equal opportunity for all. This promise had been made real to children with disabilities with the passage of the 1975 landmark federal legislation now encompassed in the Individuals with Disabilities Education Act (IDEA). Public schools across the country today serve more than six million youngsters with a wide array of disabling conditions. Reauthorizations of IDEA have committed the federal government to pay 40 percent of the average per student cost for every special education student. This is a significant commitment, as the average annual cost per special education student is over $16,000, more than $9,000 above the cost for other students.

IDEA opened up business opportunities for alternative education schools successfully dealing with special education. Among the leaders in this space are Ombudsman Educational Services was founded by Lori Sweeney and the late Jim Boyle in 1975. Ombudsman was aquired by Educational Services of America (ESA) based in Nashville, Tennessee, in 2005.

Total Education Solutions is the leading national provider of outsourcing special education compliance and staffing solutions to public education. Total Education Solutions was founded by Nancy Lavelle, who was also a former president of the Association of Educators in Private Practice, the predecessor to the Education Industry Association.

THE ASSOCIATION COMMUNITY

The outcome of the Supplemental Educational Services (SES) provisions of the No Child Left Behind Act (2001) enabled some of the service providers to become more clearly defined. The Education Industry Association seized the opportunity and established a separate SES division to serve entrepreneurs and businesses serving the half million students participating in afterschool SES programs. In addition, EIA, under the effective leadership of Executive Director Steve Pines and President Alan Carter, created a code of ethics standards for its members to respond to criticisms of SES providers and to make certain its members understood their public responsibilities. These efforts to develop industry ethics and mutual oversight were all positive signs of a maturing industry.

Associations serving other sectors of the industry also became more clearly defined. The most prominent was the Career College Association (CCA), which serves the higher education market. The CCA provided valuable lobbying and public relations communication to its members in the for-profit higher education markets. CCA has helped transform the image of for-profit colleges and universities from the stereotype of vocational and trade schools that were not taken seriously, to the reality that many were important and accredited schools of learning granting academic degrees. The CCA has made significant contributions to its membership by actively and effectively supporting the Higher Education Act. They have been particularly effective on the 90/10 rule and helping increase the availability and amount of Pell Grants. The rule requires colleges to obtain 10 percent or more of their revenues from non-federal sources in order to participate in federal student-aid programs. The public perception of some of the for-profit high schools was also affected by adverse publicity regarding some abuses of student loan policies. CCA again addressed the problems and was able to respond and communicate effectively for its members, while improving the credibility of the industry for accepting its responsibilities and, in effect, "cleaning up its act."

The Software and Information Industry Association (SIIA) also became an important trade association for the publishers and some of the early stage education-technology companies in the industry. SIIA was established through a merger of Software Publishers Association and Information Industry Associations. Its education division hosts an annual event to bring entrepreneurs and early stage investors together.

The National Council of Education Providers (NCEP) was created to provide schooling choice and options to communities that provide public funds for charter schools. The charter school members wanted to get their message out that they provided additional options. Some of the original members of NCEP were K-12, Edison, Charter USA Schools, Insight Schools, and National Heritage Academies. In addition, Jim Kohlmoos founded the National Education Knowledge Industry Association (NEKIA) to advocate support of research-based school improvement programs administered by the U.S. Department of Education.

To complete the list is National Independent Private Schools Association (NIPSA) founded in 1983 by a group of California School owners, NIPSA addresses the unique challenges and opportunities inherent in proprietary school operation.

After the passage of No Child Left Behind, the Bush administration, in an effort to define itself more clearly as a market-oriented administration, had created a separate office for education innovation. The Office of Innovation and Improvement is a nimble entrepreneurial arm of the U.S. Department of Education. It makes strategic investments in innovative educational practices through two dozen discretionary grant programs and coordinates the public school choice and supplemental education services provided by the Elementary and Secondary Education Act as amended by No Child Left Behind. It also serves as the Department's liaison to the non-education community. The Office of Innovative Improvement was originally directed by Nina Rees, who is now the senior vice president of Strategic Initiatives at Knowledge Universe.

As a leading trade association covering the education industry, EIA and its executive director, Steve Pines, and its president, Alan Carter have dealt with many thorny political issues. One of the interesting membership policy issues they wrestled with related to for-profits versus not-for-profit status. Should the EIA only be for for-profit companies? Should it only be for not-for-profit companies? In the end, through healthy discussion and debate, we determined that market-driven enterprises, whether chartered as for-profit or not-for-profit, would be welcome members of EIA, judged not on their tax status but on their core values. The board ultimately approved the core values of the EIA as follows:

- Education is a public good—all children should have access to education of the highest quality.
- Education is made better and more widely available by offering consumers' options and letting them select those that best meet their needs.

The Education Industry Association works to expand educational opportunities and improve student achievement for learners of all ages by infusing American education with market-based drivers of service, innovation, and results. In 2001, EIA sponsored its first "Education Industry Days" event with the goal of allowing members to meet with education policy leaders, legislators, and legislative staff of those government representatives who are closely aligned with the most important legislation affecting the education industry, including No Child Left Behind and its SES provisions, the Higher Education Act, and IDEA legislation.

The hosts of this event beyond the EIA are representatives of various lobbying firms that cover the education industry. These sponsors are not necessarily partisan, although more are Republicans, but recently the lobbying firms have intentionally hired people from both parties to help them advocate for education reform without the baggage of partisanship. While the EIA is an advocacy group and not a lobbying group, it serves as an industry spokesperson. The EIA's executive director and members are often called upon for testimony in pending legislation.

To support EIA, I agreed to fund an annual award for a business or government leader whose work has contributed to the mission of the Education Industry Association. The award given is called "The Friend of the Education Industry Award." Some of the recipients of the award have included David Kearns, Congressman Buck McKeon, former U.S. Secretary of Education and U.S. Senator Lamar Alexander (TN), Congressman George Miller, and former U.S. Secretary of Education Margaret Spellings.

LOBBYING FIRMS

Another example of an established structure supporting the education industry comes in the form of major law firms in Washington, DC and their advocacy support groups, who clearly see the education industry as an opportunity that is no longer fleeting, but a focused and important area for their education practice. There are numerous head hunting firms dedicated to the education industry, including Heidrick and Struggles and Korn Ferry. In recent years, former directors of communication at education companies have brought their own talent to the table. Such an example would be Steve Drake, formerly with Sylvan Learning, who has established a public relations and communications company for education entrepreneurs.

The significant policy and legislative activity not only created opportunities for education entrepreneurs but also for the legal community. Some important legislation that directly impacted education included the Individuals with Disabilities Education Act (IDEA) legislation and, of course, the Higher Education Act. Each of these elements of legislation had their own constituency, but also created opportunities for the education industry. Legislation support groups working to bring new ideas to the table and achieve implementation included Dutko, Chartwell, WilmerHale (Wilmer Cutler Pickering Hale& Dorr), the Podesta Group, and the Van Scoyoc Group.

Kaufman, Pattee & Nelson was founded by Ron Kaufman and Craig Pattee. Craig was the chief of staff for David Kearns at the Department of Education. The firm recently merged with the Dutko Group. The Dutko Group today has a significant, worldwide education practice, which is led by Craig Pattee, Gene Hickok, and Ben Wallerstein.

Chartwell was founded by former Secretary of Education Rod Paige and his chief of staff John Danielson, and the firm has an office in Washington. The firm is more consultative and globally focused. They also have an office in London and have recently been involved in the opening of private schools in the Middle East particularly in Qatar.

The law firms of Wilmer, Cutler, Pickering, Hale & Dorr and Van Scoyoc Associates round out the list of players in the lobbying space. Jay Urwitz directs WilmerHale's education services and practice. Jay has been extensively involved with the education market and worked closely with the Appropriations Committee in Health, Education and Labor before joining WilmerHale. Jay also worked with the late-Senator Ted Kennedy and was helpful in the bipartisan efforts of the passage of the No Child Left Behind legislation. Darcy Philips heads the education practice of Van Scoyoc, an association comprised of former legislative aides who had worked extensively on education legislation.

All of these groups participated in the EIA's "Education Industry Days" events. These events provided education entrepreneurs an "inside the beltway" prospective which translated into significant benefits for their companies.

CORPORATE INITIATIVES

William Symonds, the most recent Sandler fellow at Harvard's Kennedy School, has documented that education has become the number one cause supported by corporate foundations. In 2007, these foundations collectively gave about $1 billion to education. Moreover, corporations provide far more than money. "The single most important thing that business leaders can do is to encourage their employees to get involved in the schools," said former IBM CEO Lou Gerstner. IBM, for example, figures that more than 75,000 of its employees contribute over five million hours of volunteer time a year—and that more than half of this time is directed at helping the schools.

Business has also become an increasingly influential voice in shaping national education policy; after all, these are the eventual "employers" of the product of these schools. Businesses will eventually attract, retain, and sustain these students in their adult employment. The business community played a major role in lobbying Congress to pass the No Child Left Behind law in late 2001. Business leaders from all sectors assembled to create the Business Coalition for Excellence in Education, an umbrella group that included some ninety different trade associations, business groups, and companies. And in many ways, NCLB was the culmination of the standards movement, which business helped spearhead in the 1990s. In 1996, IBM CEO Lou Gerstner hosted a National Education Summit that brought together more than forty governors and nearly fifty CEOs. This Summit set the goal that every state should raise its standards, improve assessments, and strengthen its accountability standards. The 1996 Summit also established Achieve, an organization chaired by CEOs and governors, to help lead this revolution. Achieve is still very active today.

But the impact of business clearly extends far beyond standards and assessments. In recent years, leading CEOs and companies have worked to address alarming shortcomings in the teaching of the so-called STEM subjects (science, technology, engineering, and math). Another group of business leaders has been aggressively working to expand and improve early childhood education. And some of America's most prominent business leaders have helped expand the nation's network of charter schools. The Walton Family Foundation, created by Wal-Mart founder Sam Walton, has helped support charter schools in more than two-dozen urban districts, plus Arkansas. And GAP and Goldman Sachs have provided considerable support to the well-known KIPP Academies (Knowledge is Power Program), a non-profit network of charter schools that have achieved impressive results. A number of other companies—such as Ernst & Young—have helped start and support individual charter schools.

More recently, companies and corporate leaders have been working to convince schools to broaden their focus beyond such basics as math and reading to the skills students will need to succeed in the 21st century. The Partnership for 21st Century Skills has launched a campaign to persuade states to equip students with a much broader range of skills, ranging from core academics to use of information technology and life and career skills. The Partnership has grown to include such prominent companies as Microsoft, Apple, Ford, and Pearson.

Despite the current economic crisis, business must play an even bigger role in education policy and practice in the years ahead. The stakes have never been larger. If we cannot meet our education challenges, our future economic health—as well as the American Dream—will be jeopardized. It is encouraging in that as the needs grow, corporate America has responded more systemically by addressing these needs framed in the context of the skills needed by students to compete and succeed in today's world.

SUSTAINABILITY ACHIEVED

The education industry has clearly been developing upon a firm foundation created in spite of the flight of venture capitalists from the for-profit education market. The charter school movement continues to flourish in the hands of education entrepreneurs and the new and important role of their foundation partners. It is a high priority for the Obama Administration under Secretary of Education Arne Duncan. The supplemental education and tutoring services (SES) group of the Education Industry Association is a thriving group. The corporate sector, as pointed out by Bill Symonds, has developed a clear agenda for support of K-12 education reform for the 21st century. Secretary Duncan, in his prior work in Chicago as superintendent of schools, is familiar with the work of the Education Industry Association and. in fact, had been a tutor himself working with his mother in her after-school program on the south side of Chicago.

With the benefit of distance and time away for reflection, I was even more confident that because all the essential components of a sustainable structure were present, the education industry was firmly in place. Validation is nourishment for hungry and ambitious entrepreneurs. A foundation for an education market is in place, and it is one increasingly based on the understanding that private ventures for the public good are not only possible, but are sustainable and scalable.

Chapter 9

Education Entrepreneurs Responding to the Call

Chapter 9 gives the reader the opportunity to put a face on the social entrepreneurs who left their indelible mark on the education industry. The chapter illustrates the importance of their innovative enterprises and shows how they used private resources to find lasting solutions for some of education's greatest challenges. They are the people who built the imprint of the education industry today. This chapter foreshadows that with a foundation in place, through the efforts of social entrepreneurs and others, America has shown its will and potential to compete in a global knowledge economy.

There were two transformative events affecting investment in the nascent education industry during the boom-and-bust period in 1999–2000. The first was the impact of the Internet bubble bursting and the failure of online product companies and portals that were positioned as education businesses. These new ventures were consumer oriented and did not successfully facilitate the actual process of teaching and learning. The second was the failure of Edison Schools as a viable and scalable company in the public markets. Nevertheless, a new breed of education entrepreneurs remained committed to the cause and found ways to move forward despite the void of venture capital in the K-12 market. These entrepreneurs each had a vision and would not take "no" for an answer. Where doors closed, they looked for open windows of opportunity. This is what entrepreneurs do.

Education entrepreneurs over the past twenty-five years have had a significant impact on improving educational opportunities for children, and their stories needed to be told. They have been the pioneers who took huge risks to pave the way for others. They are the education entrepreneurs who demonstrated, through their careers and commitment, that a private venture could indeed be for the public good. There are many lessons to be learned from these trailblazers who possessed the courage and commitment to open doors, and windows. They provided a clearer path of opportunities for today's education entrepreneurs. There have also been a significant number of these pioneers who have had demonstrated success with their enterprises and have done well by doing good.

Educational entrepreneurship can manifest in many ways—as shown by John Dunlop, John Silber, and David Kearns. Each is unique in style and substance. John Dunlop was a coalition builder. He had a tremendous capacity to assess, understand, and ultimately resolve complex problems and issues. He was revered at Harvard by everyone from those in the janitorial service to top administrators. The ability to build trust and confidence serves educational entrepreneurs particularly well in the highly publicized, highly politicized world of education, where there are deeply vested public and private interests, and the formation of diverse coalitions is often necessary. John Dunlop sadly passed away in October of 2003. While a great loss, his legacy continues.

John Silber was a visionary. He was strong-willed and zealous, with a singular focus on improving the Chelsea Public School system. Genuinely motivated by a deep commitment to help the students and residents of Chelsea, Silber skillfully utilized his resources at Boston University to help improve education opportunities for children. His style and the boldness of the initiative sometimes drove adversaries to misunderstand the importance of his work. Undaunted by those who questioned his motives, his vision remained focused on the future. He approached the project in an entrepreneurial fashion, seeing it as a learning laboratory, with an eye to possible replication in other communities.

David Kearns was an inspirational leader who recognized the importance of research and development. During his tenure at the Department of Education, he advocated for greater research done on best practices for school improvement. He was able to use the establishment of New American Schools as a laboratory for "break the mold" school designs, supporting a complete programmatic redesign of public schools that would employ the best and the brightest teachers and innovative initiatives. New American Schools, which attracted over 600 design applications from many of the best and brightest educators and practitioners, succeeded as a catalyst for school design improvement.

These men exemplified in their own ways the traits necessary for success in building entrepreneurial enterprises in education. All three believed improvement in education was attainable, but recognized that results would come neither easily nor quickly. Other shared characteristics include:

- an everlasting belief in the American dream
- roots in education combined with a passionate commitment to improving education
- deep belief that the success of America was dependent on improvement in education

- an optimistic attitude with a dose of reality
- a thirst for knowledge
- the ability to build coalitions

CHARACTERISTICS OF EDUCATION ENTREPRENEURS

Defining the impact of private ventures for the public good in education is impossible without first taking into consideration those who laid the foundation upon which their successors now build.

Beyond being risk takers, a prerequisite for all entrepreneurs, these earliest education entrepreneurs were persistent, focused, and, most often, willing to listen and learn from others. There is distinct value for entrepreneurs who are willing to learn from mentors. Mentors make the entrepreneurial process easier, helping the entrepreneurs refine business models that otherwise might not succeed. Change in education is slow, requiring entrepreneurs to be patient. David Kearns often used the analogy that changing education "was like trying to turn the Queen Mary around."

The most successful entrepreneurs in education are creative and innovative. They have a compelling vision and possess a driving passion. Because entrepreneurs tend to have a natural curiosity, they most often question current practices, procedures, and methods in ways that trigger innovation. They see every obstacle as an opportunity and attempt to turn every setback into an advantage. Education entrepreneurs must possess these traits, enriched by a true belief and commitment to education that can help see them over tremendous hurdles.

Education offers challenges distinct from other industries—a reality that attracts some entrepreneurs and repels others. Everything takes longer and costs more than anticipated. Many potential entrants to the sector are inhibited from entering because they recognize and fear these challenges. Nevertheless, for those willing to endure an often bumpy ride, success in education can be not merely financially rewarding, but also extremely fulfilling personally.

Educational entrepreneurs have had to exhibit the tough discipline needed to succeed in a demanding market. When reviewing business plans or ideas with emerging entrepreneurs, certain questions require answers before forging ahead:

- Do they have a business plan or is it just an idea?
- Is it proprietary?
- Do they have a team committed to build and operate the enterprise?

- Can they articulate and demonstrate their commitment for the long haul?
- Do they have the staying power in terms of time and money?
- Do they have that "entrepreneurial" fire in their belly?

Only after answering questions like these with clarity and conviction should entrepreneurs proceed to the specifics of their plan, its market opportunity, and the niche that they are entering, defining its size and potential.

Certain entrepreneurs have been able to meld personal traits of success with business discipline, demonstrate a market need, and ultimately launch successful enterprises. None of their successes came easily, but despite many obstacles and barriers they prevailed. Their stories and accomplishments will stand the test of time. Some were visionaries and built significant businesses that covered various sectors of education; others focused exclusively on K-12 education and its most urgent needs. Some dealt exclusively with children at risk and those with special needs, while others navigated in the higher education and adult-learner markets. Still others came from academe and government and skillfully integrated themselves within the education industry to form associations and other industry-support enterprises.

THE TRAILBLAZERS

These well known entrepreneurs are considered pioneers of the industry who have left an indelible impact on education. They are the best examples of education entrepreneurs whose work in a nascent industry has generated a lasting impact for the public good.

- Wendy Kopp. The creator of a national core of over 7,000 recent college graduates who committed two years to teach and to effect change in under-resourced urban and rural public schools, Wendy Kopp, has created what has become known as the "Peace Corps" for American education. Wendy and her Teach for America corps and over 18,000 alumni have created a lasting legacy for social entrepreneurs.
- Deborah McGriff. After a successful career as superintendent of the Detroit public school system, Deborah joined the Edison Schools Corporation as an officer in the area of communications and public relations. While with Edison, Deborah became the president of the Education Industry Association. She helped increase the organizations membership and visibility with the K-12 school districts. Deborah is now a partner at NewSchools Ventures Fund. Deborah's husband, Howard Fuller, former superintendent

in Milwaukee, is a transformative leader in education and a longtime advocate of educational choices as a means to provide equal opportunity for all children.

- Kim Smith. The founder of the first and largest social venture fund to transform public education by supporting education entrepreneurs, Kim Smith set the tone for a whole new movement of social entrepreneurs and the effective and productive use of philanthropy for education reform. With the launching of NewSchools Venture Fund, Kim balanced intense focus on improving education with an innate skill of identifying education entrepreneurs who could create and build successful enterprises.

- Chris Whittle. A founder of the largest group of for-profit K-12 schools in America, Edison Schools, Chris Whittle has been there from the beginning. With a vision for a large scale chain of charter schools, he stuck to his founding principles, continuously refined his business model, and staked his name and reputation to advance education opportunities for all. Chris's commitment and dedication will have a lasting impact on America's inner city schools.

DOING WELL BY DOING GOOD

This next group of education entrepreneurs, although considered pioneers, also built substantial enterprises. They possessed the vision and tenacious focus to persist. Their ventures exhibited some of the most successful examples of scale and profitability within the education industry.

- Doug Becker. A founder of one of the nation's largest tutoring businesses, Doug Becker transformed Sylvan Learning into an international company, reaching over 200,000 students worldwide. In 1998, he created Laureate Education to address the post-secondary market. Laureate Education is the global leader in adult education in over sixteen countries with campuses in the Americas, Europe, and Asia. With over two decades of focused work and nimble and resourceful innovation, Doug and his business partner Chris Hoen Saric have become widely recognized as leading founders of the worldwide for-profit education market.

- Linda Mason and Roger Brown. An entrepreneurial husband and wife team that created the largest chain of work-site childcare and early education centers in America, Linda Mason and Roger Brown founded Bright Horizons Family Solutions. They created the opportunity for families to have safe, quality, early education opportunities for their children while they were at work. Roger, a lifelong music enthusiast, has also produced a number of children's music albums and most recently has become the president of Berklee School of Music in Boston. Linda was a co-director of Save the Children Relief in Sudan and worked on the border of Thailand with Cambodian refugees for UNICEF.

- Jonathan Greyer. The former chairman and CEO of a Kaplan Education, company built from a small test preparation business into a multi-billion dollar enterprise that operates dozens of colleges and an online law school. For seventeen years, Jonathan Greyer built on the strong brand that Stanley Kaplan had created by providing learning opportunities and advancement in society and careers for hundreds of thousands of people worldwide. The secret of Kaplan's success under Greyer's leadership has been their constant pursuit of systematic growth, combined with flexibility and focus on innovation. Greyer created Kaplan University with accredited online schools in the arts and sciences, business and management, education, health sciences, information systems, legal studies, and nursing. Kaplan has become a disciplined team-building organization and is now the single largest business unit within its parent company, the *Washington Post.*

- Elliot Sainer. The founder of the largest chain of boarding schools, residential treatment centers, and wilderness programs for troubled teenagers and pre-adolescent children in the United States, Sainer has provided new opportunities for troubled teens and their families. As founder and CEO of Aspen Education Group, Elliott started his career in healthcare, and after being introduced to troubled youths, wanted to help them on a bigger scale. A big picture thinker and a disciplined manager, Elliot saw the need and seized the opportunity to consolidate a significant market opportunity.

- John Sperling. One of the founders of the online higher-education market, he established the largest for-profit university in the world with over 350,000 students. Sperling is the "father" of flexible, part-time higher education opportunities for the working adult. The CEO of the University of Phoenix, John is considered a maverick and contrarian for persevering against regulation and the "system" to gain accreditation and acceptance for his university. Sperling has provided opportunities and a new lease on life for hundreds of thousands of adult learners.

SERIAL ENTREPRENEURS

Another category of committed and effective education entrepreneurs are the "romantics," who could only be described as serial entrepreneurs. They are the young breed of entrepreneurs who have gone from developing one successful education enterprises to another after catching the "the education reform bug."

- Alan Tripp. Tripp made a career of enhancing student motivation, success, and achievement. As founder and CEO of InsideTrack, his attention is now focused on the success of college students, as reflected in academic performance, persistence, and graduation rates. Previously, Alan helped launch SCORE! Education Centers, a national system of K-12 centers aimed at helping students strengthen their academic skills ands love for learning. Alan was also a lecturer at the Stanford Graduate Schools of Business and Education from 1999–2004, where he cotaught the core course for education entrepreneurs.
- John Katzman. Katzman is the founder of The Princeton Review, and a leading authority on the test-preparation market. The Princeton Review, a test preparation company, prepares students for a wide range of standardized tests (including the SAT, ACT, GMAT, GRE, LSAT, and MCAT). Following the sale of his company, John established 2tor, Inc., a private company that partners with preeminent institutions of higher education to deliver rigorous, selective degree programs online, including professional development. In 2008, Katzman established an endowed chair with the University of Southern California, designed to help reinvent what it means to be a K-12 school in the 21st century.
- Michael Koffler. The founder of Claremont Preparatory School, which is now one of the largest private schools in New York City, was established shortly after September 11, one block from Ground Zero. Michael Koffler saw early on the market need for good schools in lower Manhattan and Brooklyn. He is considered a leading contributor to the rebuilding of life in these communities. Michael remains undaunted in his tireless efforts to provide support to parents with children who suffer with autism spectrum disorders through his Aaron and Rebecca schools, which were established after the opening of the Claremont Preparatory School. Michael began his serial educational entrepreneurial career operating special needs programs within a group of schools in New York. He then went on to establish the Claremont Children's School, a pre-school on the West Side of New York City.
- Rob Waldron. Ron is the current president and COO of Curriculum Associates, a leading publisher of research-based material for diverse classroom settings. Before joining Curriculum Associates, he was president and CEO of Jumpstart, a not-for-profit company focused on early childhood education. In 2004, while at Jumpstart, Rob created a new initiative, School Readiness For All, which was established to help prepare at-risk children

for school success. Prior to Jumpstart, Rob was one of the original founders of SCORE! Learning Centers, which merged with Kaplan Education.

NEW BREED OF LEADERSHIP

The for-profit higher education market has become a significant sector of the U.S. economy and is poised for long-term growth and profitability. In fact, during the stock market meltdown in late 2008 and early 2009, the for-profit higher education stocks were among the leading performers.

Confident founders who had the foresight to attract professional managers have "transferred" the leadership of their companies to professional managers, which assures continuity of the vision they have for their company. These managers hail from the highest echelon in their fields, such as that of law, business, government, and consulting.

A good example of this new breed of professional manager is Daniel Hamburger, president and CEO of DeVry. Before becoming CEO, Hamburger had served as COO since 2002. Prior to joining DeVry, he was the chairman and CEO of Indeliq, now owned by Accenture Learning, and has also worked at Bain Consulting. With a solid background in consulting and strategic thinking, Daniel has built DeVry into an industry leader in both higher education and, recently, the K-12 market.

In 2001, a private equity group, New Mountain Capital, acquired control of Strayer Education, Inc, a company originally founded in 1892 as a secretarial school. Following the acquisition, they recruited Rob Silberman to lead Strayer. Under Rob's guidance and leadership, Strayer has become a highly regarded company in higher education with a market value in excess of $2.5 billion. Prior to joining Strayer, Silberman was CEO of CalEnergy Company and, earlier, International Paper Company. Silberman has also held several senior positions in the U.S. Department of Defense.

Andrew Rosen was named chairman and CEO of Kaplan, Inc. in November 2008, succeeding CEO Jonathan Greyer. In 2002, Andrew was named president of Kaplan and assumed responsibility for all of Kaplan's higher education operations, including Kaplan University, Concord Law School, and Kaplan Virtual Education. Rosen previously served as Kaplan's COO. Rosen came to The Washington Post Company, a Kaplan subsidiary, in 1986 as a staff attorney for the newspaper. He moved to Newsweek as assistant counsel in 1988 before coming to Kaplan in 1992.

Jonathan Kaplan became president of Walden University in 2007 after serving several years as an officer of Walden University and in a range of senior positions at Laureate Education, Inc. He was trained as a lawyer and worked at the firm of Covington and Burling. Jonathan also had significant government experience as an economic policy advisor to President Bill Clinton. During his public sector career, he held posts at the U.S. Department of the Treasury and on Capital Hill, focusing on domestic and economic policy issues. Through Jon's legal and government experience, he was better prepared to become president of an international online university.

WHERE DO WE GO FROM HERE?

The last hundred years have witnessed important and dramatic economic growth that has transformed nearly every sector of the American economy—except education. Walking into a classroom from the 19th century would be strangely familiar to people today. While fashions and tools may have changed dramatically, the overall design of the classroom with the teacher in the front of the classroom and students ingesting information has remained largely intact. America has some tough choices ahead as we deal with a major economic crisis. There are those who say entrepreneurs are needed to help stimulate our economy by rebuilding our schools. Unfortunately, there is just not enough money to rebuild all our schools, while also working to improve student performance as we compete globally. The good news is that just as we begin to face some of these tough choices, we are simultaneously encouraged by the foundation pieces that have been established by education entrepreneurs.

It is no longer a question as to *whether* a permanent change can happen in the K-12 sector, but *when* it will happen, and *who* will be the key players. Few would disagree that for-profit higher education is a scalable industry sector, and, in fact, permanent market reforms in the K-12 sector have indeed taken place, though they are less visible to the untrained eye and have not quite reached the point of broad scalability.

Scale in education has it own set of criteria, different from any other sector of the economy because of its unique position as a state and local political issue, in which the federal government is becoming increasingly involved. The leaders of New American Schools were having these conversations almost twenty years ago, discussing their ability to create scale in schools with their design team models. The consensus then was that the public would become engaged by innovations in technology. While technology and laptops for all are important, they have not proven the key drivers of change. Instead, the driver has ended up being the vision, creativity, passion, and persistence of education entrepreneurs responding to market needs for innovation.

We don't know precisely when the tipping point of scalability in K-12 occurred, but the objective of this book is to effectively make the case that the necessary *foundation* for scale in the K-12 market has been attained.

Consider the following. At the time of the *A Nation At Risk* report (1983), there was an education industry of approximately $25 billion in revenues. It was comprised of companies that were creating, publishing, and distributing products to America's schools, whether textbooks , school supplies, CD-roms and software products, technology products, or supplemental educational materials. There was no addressable service market, and proprietary schools were less than a $2 billion market in the combined K-12 and post-secondary market. Since 1983, the educational products sector has consistently grown with the rate of inflation of 3–4 percent to a total of more than $50 billion in revenues. On the other hand, the schools and service markets have grown from virtually no financial base into a market of approximately $50 billion in revenues, which is close to being equally distributed between K-12 and higher education. These numbers of K-12 and higher education market do not include the $22 billion childcare market, which was miniscule in 1983.

ATTAINMENT OF SCALE

So what happened? Education entrepreneurs created a viable, sustainable, and scalable industry sector. They saw both the needs *and* the opportunities. Entrepreneurial business leaders, educators, philanthropists, and policymakers collaborated in discovering new ways to educate America's youth and train its workforce, present and future. The new charter school movement of the early 1990s was one of the early creative responses to the challenges, and the movement now encompasses 4,600 schools and 1.6 million students. Parents of homeschoolers seeking alternatives to failing schools or to instill their religious beliefs created a new demand for educational products and now comprise a market segment of 1.5 million people who directly purchase educational materials and services that are delivered to them in a variety of ways. Other parents complained of poor student performance, entrepreneurs opened tutoring centers, and now, with government support, there is an overall $3 billion school and consumer market and 500,000 students participating in school SES programs. Technology drove the online schooling success achieved in higher education and is now advancing to K-12. Entrepreneurs in the special education market addressed major societal issues of learning disabilities and social and behavioral problems, and they have created a $5 billion market serving over 300,000 students. While many investors backed off from the K-12 market to seek returns in the more easily scalable higher education market, the K-12 entrepreneurs continued to march forward.

The belief that they were joined in a common cause contributed to the persistence and dedication of these entrepreneurs, and this belief emerged in part from the fact that we began to conceive of and talk about an over-all K-12 marketplace. If you build it, they will come. Creating space for people to think in terms of a K-12 marketplace has helped provide education entrepreneurs with an identity and has fostered learning, innovations, and synergy. Education entrepreneurs have created thousands of enterprises which employ millions of professionals who deal with the important educational issues of child care, tutoring, after-school programs, online schools, charter schools, alternative and special education, and home schooling. Because of the success of these ventures, the public is now engaged and increasingly receptive to private ventures for the public good. In the various sectors they serve, education entrepreneurs have demonstrated that K-12 is an addressable and scalable industry. But there is much more work ahead.

The successful attainment of scale in many areas of the higher education market may point the way toward a proven and sustainable industry model which K-12 can emulate. There has been credible success in bringing online learning to bear in transforming higher education. There are now over 4,000 colleges and universities in the United States, a small number in comparison with the 15,000 school districts and 90,000 schools. However, the changes taking place are widespread and will be irreversible. The business of higher education has changed, and that successful innovation will continue and will influence the K-12 market as well. In fact, many of the leading for-profit higher education universities are already setting their sights on the K-12 market.

The transformation of traditional higher education is covered in detail by Peter Stokes, executive vice president of Eduventures, Inc., in a provocative issue paper written as a contribution to the national dialogue of the secretary of education's Commission on the Future of Higher Education, of which Peter was a member. *Hidden in Plain Sight: Adult Learners Forge a New Tradition in Higher Education* points out that adult learners are now the new market force in higher education. Eighteen to twenty-two year olds, the traditional undergraduate students, now make up only about 16 percent of higher education enrollment. People who still think of college as young students, campuses, and four years of dormitory life have an outdated perception of what the word "college" means these days!

Most students today are not conventional in the traditional sense. Forty percent of students are part-time, 40 percent attend two-year institutions, 40 percent are twenty-five or older, and 58 percent are twenty-two or older. The case can be made that "non-traditional" students, many of whom are juggling a job and family in addition to studying part-time, are now the new norm. Many attend community colleges, are enrolled in schools of continuing or professional education at public or private universities or, in some instances, are receiving training in the workplace. Although adult learners are everywhere in higher education, they have largely remained invisible—hidden in plain sight. With the current unemployment rate close to 10 percent, the need to train adults for new skills will continue to increase the "non-traditional" market.

Similar dramatic changes have already happened in the traditional K-12 market, but are somewhat "hidden" because K-12 is so local, political, and simply so large in terms of the specific numbers of institutions and students served. Where we once thought that scale would involve new practices or routines to be injected successfully into thousands of districts or tens of thousands of schools at once, it is more plausible that successful innovations in K-12 education ventures would require a fresh slate, starting small, and slowly carve out their share of influence in the market.

There has also been a very significant growth in online delivery of K-12 instructional programs, with over 1 million students now participating in some form of online schooling. Recently, major for-profit universities such as the University of Phoenix (Insight Schools) and DeVry's (Advanced Academics) have acquired virtual K-12 schools and are building a delivery system to the K-12 market. The Sloan Consortium (MIT research) reports significant growth in online learning among the nation's elementary and secondary school students. It is estimated that more than 1 million students are participating in online high schools and forecasts the online high school market to reach 5 million by 2014.

Thousands of independent programs and "alternative" schools are helping redefine the vital services needed for children with learning disabilities, behavioral problems, and other special needs that public schools cannot, for a number of reasons, provide. No longer is it sufficient to lump all these children together in "special education" without attending to their unique personal abilities and obstacles to learning. There has also been dramatic growth of new programs and technology platforms for vocational schools for high school dropouts. According to Ibisworld research, the market size of alternative, vocational and special education is approximately $100 billion, and approximately 5 percent or $5 billion is attributed to for-profit companies.

TOUGH CHOICES AHEAD

This book covers the quarter-century journey by entrepreneurs to build and sustain an education industry. Twenty-five years is an eternity for some—to others, a relatively small period of our nation's history.

Education is a comparably small sector of our economy, but for many reasons is arguably our most important. It is my hope that this book paints an optimistic view that somewhere below the radar screen education entrepreneurs have responded to the call of A *Nation At Risk* and created a viable education industry. With this foundation in place, there is optimism that over the next quarter century, America can regain its position as the global leader in education, continuing to successfully compete in the worldwide markets with a highly skilled labor force.

With our education industry foundation firmly in place, America now faces some tough choices. A 2007 report by the National Center on Education and The Economy, *Tough Choices or Tough Times*, chronicles these challenges. The report was written by The New Commission on the Skills of the American Workforce. The Commission was composed of the foremost experts in business and education. The Commission was chaired by Charles Knapp, director of Education Development, CF Foundation, and president emeritus, University of Georgia. The vice chairman and staff director of the Commission was Marc S. Tucker, president of the National Center on Education and the Economy. Some of the notable members of the Commission included John Engler, Steve Gunderson, Joel Klein, Thomas Payzant, Richard Riley, and Henry Schacht. *Tough Choices* is a follow up report to one published in 1990, *America's Choice: HighSkills or Low Wages.* Today, many leaders in business, government, and education consider the *Tough Choices or Tough Times* report a descendant of the A *Nation At Risk* report in 1983.

Tough Choices argues that to be competitive in today's global markets, high levels of preparation in reading, writing, speaking, mathematics, science, literature, history, and the arts are necessary for most members of the workforce. The best employers worldwide are looking for the most competent, creative, and innovative employees and are willing to pay them top dollar for their services. Because of the flattening of the marketplace, this will be true not just for the top professionals and managers, but at all levels of the workforce. *Tough Choices* further argues that our core problem is that America's education and training systems were built for another era. To adapt the system to get to where we need to be will require a near full overhaul of the system itself. It is around this archaic system that education entrepreneurs built a viable industry over the past twenty-five years.

Going forward, President Obama and his administration have focused on education as one of their highest priorities, allocating $100 billion of the $787 billion 2009 economic stimulus bill to education. This is more than double the current annual budget of the Department of Education. Both the *Tough Choices* report and the economic stimulus bill identify that the solutions will come from innovation and creative solutions, which is the signal for entrepreneurs to step forward once again. Because so much money is being injected into the system, those who can offer innovative solutions to market needs or gaps have the opportunity to be well rewarded if they can execute these solutions successfully. Also within the budget, Education Secretary Arne Duncan has created a separate discretionary fund of $5 billion for district superintendents around the country for innovative and transformative solutions for our education challenges.

It is my hope that the experiences and lessons of education entrepreneurs will inform superintendents, principals, teachers, and all stakeholders in education that private ventures can serve both shareholders and students in education. It is also intended to validate the tireless efforts of the tens of thousands of education entrepreneurs who have toiled in the past twenty-five years. Not only have they created viable enterprises employing millions, they have made a lasting contribution to the education of countless students. Finally, since Americans are a restless breed, I hope this inspires the reader that with the right characteristics you, too, can "hang a shingle" and become an education entrepreneur.

While full of optimism, we are still a nation at risk. But through thoughtful innovation and some tough choices, we can build on the foundation of our education entrepreneurs and prevail with an education system of which we can all be proud.

Epilogue

BASEBALL, EDUCATION AND OUR FUTURE

My favorite place in the world is Fenway Park, where I root for my team, the Boston Red Sox. There are many reasons to love Fenway Park and the Red Sox; my devotion comes from knowing that baseball teaches practical life lessons.

Baseball is not a boring game: it's subtle, like life. It is a truly American game that can tie one generation to the next. As the eminent historian Jacques Barzun wrote: "Whoever wants to know the heart and mind of America, had better learn baseball." It's about history, diversity, math, and statistics. While the look of both schools and baseball fields seem to have remained mostly unchanged over the last fifty years, the fact is that they have both changed in less obvious ways.

Baseball's many lessons teach both broad life lessons and ones more specific to other topics, including education. My friend Steve Ealy publishes an annual "What Price per Victory Survey" for baseball fans, based on data provided by CBS Sports. In 2008, the team with the highest payroll expenditure in Major League Baseball was the New York Yankees ($209,081,579), fourth was the Boston Red Sox ($133,440,037) and twenty-ninth, the Tampa Bay Rays ($29,836,500). That season, the Yankees won 89 games and the Rays 84, meaning the Yankees paid $37,440,015 for each five additional wins.

Tampa Bay, with the second-lowest payroll in baseball, won the American League Championship Series and made it to the World Series (where they ultimately lost to the Phillies), proving that money alone does not guarantee a winning performance.

The same can be said for education. When John Silber was running for governor of Massachusetts, he would often remark that if you want a mediocre education, you could go to Chelsea and pay half the price to get the same education you could get in Boston. At that time, Chelsea and Boston were recognized as peers at the lowest category of student performance measurement in the Commonwealth.

Why is more money not necessarily better in baseball or education? The answer is one of innovation—a matter of looking at the same statistics and evidence in a new way. For our students to be truly competitive in the 21st century, traditional K-12 education needs more competition and an open environment for entrepreneurs to address serious policy issues, including student performance, merit pay, school choice, and teacher tenure. Some of the best remedies for education are available through competition in the marketplace; more money does not necessarily improve performance.

Today, the political climate is embracing change, not just in education. The Obama administration is braced to persuade teachers to join those seeking greater accountability. It is the right time and opportunity to rally teachers and unions to support performance pay. Improving education is at the forefront of improving our economy. We need many incentives (including financial) for improved performance; likewise, for those who do not perform, we should take a cue from baseball and either sign for less money or be willing to enhance skills by transferring to the education equivalent of the instructional level of the minor leagues.

Through the efforts of education entrepreneurs and others, dramatic changes have taken place in American education over the past twenty-five years. Where will the next wave of educational entrepreneurship take us? Revised funding models and the role of government, the advent of learning via social networking (Web 2.0 and beyond), and the continued importance of anywhere/anytime, lifelong learning in a global, knowledge economy will all shape its form.

Few would have imagined that in late 2008 and 2009 the U.S. government would become the lender of last resort to a number of "too large to fail" institutions to keep our economies from collapsing. If any institution in the United States is "too large to fail," it is the education system. It is time to give our teaching professionals the same support we give those in the financial and automotive sectors. Yet, the economic credit and global market crisis has redefined the role of government across a range of industries.

In the current climate, the role of government in education has been most visible as it has essentially "doubled down" its investment in education, openly calling for entrepreneurial innovation and capital investment. Because of this, it seems likely that venture capitalists will return in droves. With government as a strong advocate and the opportunities abundant, venture investing will flourish once again. This is an important and encouraging outcome, as venture capitalists use innovation as the basis for their decision making.

Another call for innovation was emphasized in the 2007 *Tough Choices or Tough Times* report from the New Commission on the Skills of the American Workforce. This report clearly shows that high-skill, high-wage jobs represent America's economic future, and it calls for a complete overhaul of U.S. education by 2021. These are good times for education entrepreneurs. The government, venture capitalists, and philanthropists are focused on social entrepreneurship and education as major priorities.

We are fortunate that during these challenging times, we are blessed with Internet technologies that did not exist ten years ago. Between the social learning needs and willing investors, the opportunities and capital are abundant for entrepreneurs.

Education is a bipartisan issue—we all care equally and deeply about the sad state of our schools. The time is ripe for a new administration to tear down those barriers and convince our teachers' unions that performance and merit pay are long overdue. We have attacked our outmoded automobile industry by facing down deep-rooted challenges from labor and management. We are doing the same with regard to the environment, healthcare, and energy. Why not seize this opportunity for change in education?

The past twenty-five years in the education industry reveal much about who we are as a nation:

- We are an aspiring nation–entrepreneurs have created after-school enterprises that support working families and their children by combining childcare, tutoring, and coaching to help advance and support their future.
- We are a caring and nurturing nation—entrepreneurs found opportunities to assist those at risk with learning disabilities and increasing challenges such as autism.
- We are an innovative nation—entrepreneurs used the Internet to deliver courses to adult and young learners and to redefine what it meant to be a student at any time and place.
- We are a competitive nation—charter schools and organizations such as Teach for America help all of us improve ourselves by raising the bar of success.

Like most people who were born and bred in northern New England—that is, Red Sox Nation—I understood what my father meant when he would say, "Good luck to you and the Red Sox." The Red Sox had not won a World

Series since 1918, when my dad was 10. They always came close . . . but consistently let us down. When he would tell me "Good luck to you and the Red Sox"—usually in response to some crazy idea I might have—it was his way of saying that he didn't see it happening, but he wanted to motivate and not discourage me. Like others who became Red Sox fans at a young age, I consequently became a strong advocate for the underdog and entrepreneurship.

"Good luck to you and the Red Sox" has been my motivating mantra in professional and personal life. I was determined to succeed at whatever I set my mind to do . . . and the Red Sox were going to win the World Series one day. This ideal drove my persistence and perseverance—key attributes for education entrepreneurs. For their part, after an eighty-six year drought, the Red Sox won the first of their two World Series in three years in 2004.

Somehow, somewhere, we have lost our competitive edge in education. But it doesn't have to be "Good luck to you, the U.S. education system, and the Red Sox." The past twenty-five years, coupled with the optimism and thirst for change in this era, have shown that these original education entrepreneurs were on target and that the notion that private ventures for the public good could provide the foundation piece that we could continue to build upon for generations to come. As a nation now truly at risk, the incentives and opportunities are aligned. The positive response of social entrepreneurs in education will be heard loud and clear.

Bibliography

Except where specifically mentioned, the quotes in this book are drawn from the author's interviews or author articles, research previously published by Eduventures Inc., education industry research investment reports, the annual reports of A Different September Foundation and New American Schools, and the publications of the Education Industry Association (which includes its Career Guide and Education Industry Leadership Report). All financial transactions were verified by public information and from the Web sites of the companies mentioned. Particularly informative sources are listed in the Additional Resources list.

A Different September Foundation Annual Report. 1991.

Applebome, Peter. "Lure of the Education Market Remains Strong for Business." *New York Times,* January 31, 1996.

Benavidis, Lisa. "For-Profit Education Creating Big Business." *Boston Business Journal,* January 10, 1997.

BMO Capital Markets Back to School Annual Report 2007. Accessed at: www.bmo .com/conferences/backtoschool.

BMO Capital Markets Back to School Annual Report 2008. Accessed at: www.bmo .com/conferences/backtoschool.

BMO Capital Markets Back to School Annual Report 2009. Accessed at: www.bmo .com/conferences/backtoschool.

Botsford, Keith. "Chelsea Schools—The Who's, How's and Why's Behind Boston University's Experimental Management of that City's School System." *Bostonia,* November/December 1989.

Bradley, Ann. "Chelsea Schools Reopens Amid Uncertainty Over Near-Bankrupt City's Fiscal Health." *Education Week*, September 25, 1991.

Bury, Liz. "Pearson Sees Online Future for Education," *Bookseller*, August 4, 2000.

The Center for Education Reform, "The Mandate for Change." Washington, DC, January 2009.

"Charter Success in L.A." *Wall Street Journal editorial*, October 14, 2008.

Eduventures Inc. 1996 Research Brief Overview

The Bill and Melinda Gates Foundation. Accessed at: www.gatesfoundation.org.

Ganem, Robert. "A Different September Foundation, The Boston Unversity/Chelsea School Partnership, Summary Of Accomplishments." November 1991.

Glader, Paul. "The Jack Welch MBA: Coming to Web." *Wall Street Journal,* June 22, 2009.

McGrory, Mary. "Wrench in a Wheel of Poverty." *Washington Post,* May 7, 1991.

Moe, Michael T. "Book of Knowledge: Investing in the Growing Education and Training Industry." A Report Prepared for Merrill Lynch, April 9, 1999.

Moe, Michael T., and Henry Blodget. "Knowledge Web: People–Fuel for the New Economy." A Report Prepared for Merrill Lynch, May 23, 2000.

Muscovitch, Edward. "Innovative Programs Make a Difference in Chelsea Schools." *Boston Herald,* July 7, 1991.

Palladino, Franca. A Different September Foundation *Newsletter VI,* no. 1, Spring 1994.

Sandler, Michael. Career Opportunities in the Education Industry. *Education Industry Association,* July 2006.

Statistics of Public School Expenditures. Published by Charles Scribner's Sons New York. Accessed at: www.davidrumsey.com.

Stokes, Peter J. "Hidden in Plain Sight: Adult Learners Forge a New Tradition in Education." 11th Paper submitted to the Secretary of Education's Commission on the Future of Higher Education, December 2, 2005.

U.S. Department of Education. *A Nation at Risk: The Imperative for Educational Reform. A Report to the Nation and the Secretary of Education,* April 1983.

Vision to Reality: the New American Schools Development Corporation Annual Report 1993–94. Alexandria, VA, 1994.

Weisman, Robert. "A New Test for Education Publisher." *Boston Globe,* January 31, 2007.

Additional Resources

ASSOCIATIONS

American Association of School Administrators (AASA), *www.aasa.org*
American Federation of Teachers (AFT), *www.aft.org*
Educause, www.educause.edu
National Association of Charter School Authorizers (NACSA), *www .qualitycharters.org*
National Association of College and University Business Officers (NACUBO), www.nacubo.org
National Association of Independent Schools (NAIS), *www.nais.org*
National Association for Year, Round Education (NAYRE), *www.nayre.org*
National Association of Secondary School Principals (NASSP), *www.nassp.org*
National Association for the Education of Young Children (NAEYC), *www.naeyc.org*
National Education Association (NEA), *www.nea.org*
National Independent Private Schools Association (NIPSA), *www.nipsa.org*
National School Boards Association (NSBA), *www.nsba.org*

TRADE ASSOCIATIONS

Association of American Publishers (AAP), *www.publishers.org*
California Charter School Association (CCSA), *www.myschool.org*
Career College Association (CCA), *www.career.org*
Education Industry Association (EIA), *www.educationindustry.org*

Independent Educational Consultants Association (IECA), *www.education-alconsulting.org*

National Council of Education Providers (NCEP), *www.educationproviders.org*

National Education Knowledge Industry Association (NEKIA), *www.nekia.org*

National School Supply and Equipment Association (NSSEA), *www.nssea.org*

Parent Teachers Association (PTA), *www.ptacentral.org*

Publishers Marketing Association (PMA), *www.pma, online.org*

Software Information and Industry Association (SIIA), www.siia.net

The Association of Educational Publishers (AEP), *www.aepweb.org*

The National Association of Therapeutic Schools and Programs (NATSAP), *www.natsap.org*

United States Distance Learning Association (USDLA), *www.usdla.org*

OTHER ORGANIZATIONS

Alternative Education Resource Organization (AERO), *www.educationrevolution.org*

American Council on Education (ACE), *www.acenet.edu*

American Distance Education Consortium (ADEC), *www.adec.edu*

American Enterprise Institute (AEI), *www.aei.org*

American Society for Training & Development (ASTD), *www.astd.org*

Ashoka, *www.ashoka.org*

Black Alliance for Educational Options (BAEO), *www.baeo.org*

Center for Education Reform (CER), *www.edreform.com*

Council of Chief State School Officers (CCSSO), *www.ccsso.org*

Council for Public, Private Partnerships (NCPPP), *www.ncppp.org*

Education Commission of the States (ECS), *www.ecs.org*

Institute of Economic Affaires (IEA), *www.iea.org.uk*

National Center for Study for Privatization in Education (NCSPE), w*ww.ncspe.org*

National Charter School Alliance, *www.publiccharters.org*

National Conference of State Legislators (NCLS), *www.ncls.org*

National Network of Partnership Schools (NNPS), *www.csos.jhu.edu/P2000*

Northwest Regional Educational Laboratories (NWREL), *www.nwrel.org*

Teachers Insurance an Annuity Association of America (TIAA-CREF), *www.tiaa, cref.org*

The College Board, *www.collegeboard.com*

The Council of Chief State School Officers (CCSSO), *www.ccsso.org*
The Sloan Consortium, *www.sloan-c.org*

FOUNDATIONS

Annenberg Foundation, *www.annenbergfoundation.org*
Bill and Melinda Gates Foundation, *www.gatesfoundation.org*
Carnegie Corporation, *www.carnegie.org*
Education Industry Foundation, www.educationindustry.org
Eli and Edythe Broad Foundation, *www.broadfoundation.org*
Ford Foundation, *www.fordfound.org*
Heritage Foundation, *www.heritage.org*
Inner City Education Foundation, *www.icefla.org*
Kaufman Foundation, *www.kauffman.org*
Milton & Rose D. Friedman Foundation, *www.friedmanfoundation.org*
Rockefeller foundation *www.rockfound.org*
Skoll Foundation, *www.skollfoundation.org*
The Milken Family Foundation, *www.mff.org*
The Pisces Foundation, *thepiscesfoundation.com*
Walton Family Foundation, *www.waltonfamilyfoundation.org*

GOVERNMENT ORGANIZATIONS

National Center for Education Statistics (NCES), *nces.ed.gov/*
National Clearinghouse for Educational Facilities (NCEF), *www.edfacilities*
    .org
Office of Innovation and Improvement (OII), *www.ed.gov/about/offices/list/oii*
U.S. Department of Education (DOE), *www.ed.gov*

TRADE PUBLICATIONS

EdNet Week Headlines, *www.hellerreports.com*
EducationNews.org
Education Week, www.edweek.org
eSchool News, *www.eschoolnews.com*
InsideHigherEd, *www.insidehighered.com*
The Chronicle of Higher Education, *chronicle.com*
T.H.E. Journal, *www.thejournal.com*
University Business, *www.universitybusiness.com*

MARKET RESEARCH AND PUBLICATIONS\

American School Directory (ASD), *www.asd.com*

A Nation At Risk, The National Commission on Excellence, *www.ed.gov/ pubs/NatAtRisk/*

Eduventures, *www.Eduventures.com*

Education Market Research (EMR), *www.educationmarketresearch.com/*

Simba Information, *www.simbainformation.com*

Career Opportunities in the Education Industry-Education Industry Association, *www.educationindustry.org*

Hidden in Plain Sight: Adult Learners Forge a New Tradition in Higher Education, Peter Stokes, Executive Vice President of Eduventures, *www .ed.gov/about/bdscomm/list/hiedfuture/reports/stokes.pdf*

Investing in Charter Schools: A Guide for Donors, Philanthropy Roundtable, *http://www.philanthropyroundtable.org/store_product.asp?prodid=218*

Market Data Retrieval (MDR), *www.schooldata.com*

The Education Industry, Special Report, The Education Industry Leadership Board, *www.educationindustry.org*

Tough Choices or Tough Times, The New Commission on Skills of the American Workforce, *skillscommission.org/executive.htm*

Quality Education Data (QED), *www.qeddata.com*

INVESTMENT RESEARCH NEWSLETTERS AND REPORTS

BMO Capital Markets, Back to School Annual Report, *www.bmocm.com*

Class Notes Newsletter: Monthly Insights on the Education Market: Robert W. Baird, *http://www.rwbaird.com*

EdInvest Newsletter, www.ifc.org/ifcext/edinvest.nsf/Content/Newsletter

Knowledge Notes Monthly Newsletter: Signal Hill, *http://www.signalhill.com/*

NeXT Up, Factbook and Newsletter, *www.nextupresearch.com*

BOOKS

Adventures of Charter School Creators: Leading from the Ground Up, Therrence E. Deal

A Legacy Of Learning: Your Stake in Standards and New Kinds of Public Schools, David T. Kearns and James Harvey (The Brookings Institution, 2000)

Crash Course: Imagining A Better Future For Public Education, Chris Whittle (Penguin Group, 2005)

Educational Entrepreneurship: Realities, Challenges, Possibilities, Frederick M. Hess

Educational Private Practice: Your Opportunity in the Changing Education Marketplace, Dennis C. Zuelke (The Scarecrow Press, Inc., 2001)

From The Ground Up: Entrepreneurial School Leadership, Jeffrey R. Cornwall (Scarecrow Press Inc., 2003)

Going Broke By Degree: Why Colleges Costs Too Much, Richard Vedder (AEI Press, 2004)

Handbook of Educational Leadership and Management, Brent Davies and John West, Burnham (Pearson Education Limited, 2003)

Higher Ed, Inc; The Rise of the For-Profit University, Richard Ruch (The Johns Hopkins University Press, 2001)

Inside Urban Charter Schools: Promising Practices and Strategies in Five High-Performing Schools, Katherine K. Merseth with Kristy Cooper, John Roberts, Mara Casey Tieken, John Valant, and Chris Wynne (Harvard Education Press, 2009)

Future of Educational Entrepreneurship: Possibilities for School Reform, Frederick M. Hess (Harvard Education Press, 2008)

Learning on the Job; When Business Takes on Public Schools, Steven Wilson (Harvard University Press, 2006)

New Players, Different Game, Guilbert Hentschke and William G. Tierney (The Johns Hopkins University Press, 2007)

One Day, All Children, Wendy Kopp (PublicAffairs, 2001) and Guilbert C. Hentschke (ScarecrowEducation, 2004)

Reclaiming Education, James Tooley (Cassel, 2000)

Rebel with a Cause, John Sperling (John Wiley & Sons, 2000)

Success, Susan C. Awe (Libraries Unlimited, 2006)

The Entrepreneurial Educator, Robert J. Brown and Jeffrey R. Cornwall (Scarecrow Press Inc., 2000)

The Educational Entrepreneur: Making A Difference, Donald E. Leisey, EdD, and Charles Lavaroni, MS (Edupreneur Press, 2000)

The Entrepreneur's Information Sourcebook: Charting the Path to Small Business Success, Susan Awe (Libraries Unlimited, 2006), *Winning the Brain Race*, David Kearns (ICS Press, 1989).

Index

Sharpe, Ted, 18
Shrontz, Frank, 28
SIIA. *See* Software and Information
   Industry Association
Silber, John, 5–7, 9–15, 19, 21, 23, 27,
   37, 126, 140
Silberman, Rob, 132
Sloan Consortium, 136
SmarterKids.com, 61–62, 71
Smith, Kim, 112, 129
Snyder, Tom, 38
social entrepreneurs, 2, 102;
   aligned expectations of, 66;
   clashes between, 74; competition
   and, 53; EduVentures.com
   attracting, 72; EduVentures
   helping, 41–42; impact of,
   125–26; key traits of, 55–56,
   126–28; learning by, 9; planning,
   flexibility and, 82; serial, 21,
   130–32; substantial enterprises
   built by, 129–30; success of, 111;
   trailblazers, 128–29
social entrepreneurship: current climate
   of, 140–41; Harvard Kennedy School
   seminar series, 5–6; public, 23;
   trendiness of, 37
Software and Information Industry
   Association (SIIA), 120
Sparkman, James, 66
Spaulding, Josiah (Joe), Jr., 5–6
Speakman, Sherry, 43
special education market, 118–19
Spellings, Margaret, 121
Sperber, Robert, 18
Sperling, John, 45, 87
Stanford University, 110–11
Steck Vaughn Publishing, 88
Steinert, Arthur, 44
Stokes, Peter, 67–68, 70, 82, 135
Stonington Partners, 87
Strayer Education, 93, 132
Success for All program, 31
succession planning, 21–23

Supplemental Education Suppliers
   (SES), 105–6, 119, 121
sustainability, 124
Sylvan Learning Systems, 40, 45–46,
   61, 88, 122, 129
Symonds, Bill, 8, 123–24

Tanner, Mary, 47
teachers' unions, 11, 41
Teach for America (TFA), 40, 112,
   115, 141
technological illiteracy, 105
Tenet Health Care, 68
TFA. *See* Teach for America
third party verification, 57
Thomson Learning, 90
three-legged stool model, 39–40
Total Education Solutions, 119
Tough Choices or Tough Times, 137–38,
   141
traditional publishing, 59–60
trailblazing entrepreneurs, 128–29
training, 60
Tripp, Alan, 131
tutoring, 61–62

United States (U.S.): advantages of, 51;
   education ideal of, 1
University of Pennsylvania, 15
University of Phoenix, 94, 130, 136
University of Southern California
   (USC), 110, 117, 131
Urwitz, Jay, 122
USA Today, 22
USC. *See* University of Southern
   California

Vander Ark, Tom, 114
venture capital: boom, 100–103;
   bust, 103–6; investors, 100–102,
   140–41
*Venture Capitalists Seek Reality,
   Revenues and Rational Business
   Models*, 103–4

About the Author

Michael R. Sandler coined the term "education industry" and is considered one of the industry's founding fathers. A lifelong entrepreneur, he has built a career both in business and education. He established Eduventures Inc. in 1993 after founding and selling several successful businesses, including Marsan Industries (which merged with ITT Corporation) and Auto Parts Distributors, (which was sold to Rite-Aid Corporation). In 1989, Sandler served as a fellow at Harvard's Kennedy School, where he conducted research on the contributions of the private sector to education. A graduate of the Wharton School at the University of Pennsylvania, Sandler has served as a trustee of the University and as an overseer of its School of Arts and Sciences. He was the founder of A Different September Foundation, an organization that supported the Boston University/Chelsea Public Schools Partnership. He is also president of the Education Industry Foundation. In 2006 and 2007, Sandler was an executive-in-residence at the University of Southern California, exploring business and education issues as they relate to access to capital and career opportunities in the education industry. Currently, Mr. Sandler is chairman and CEO of the Education Industry Group, an advisory firm supporting social entrepreneurship in education. He resides in Boston with his wife, Ellen, and they have three daughters, two sons-in-law, and four grandchildren.